CRAFT THE RAINBOW

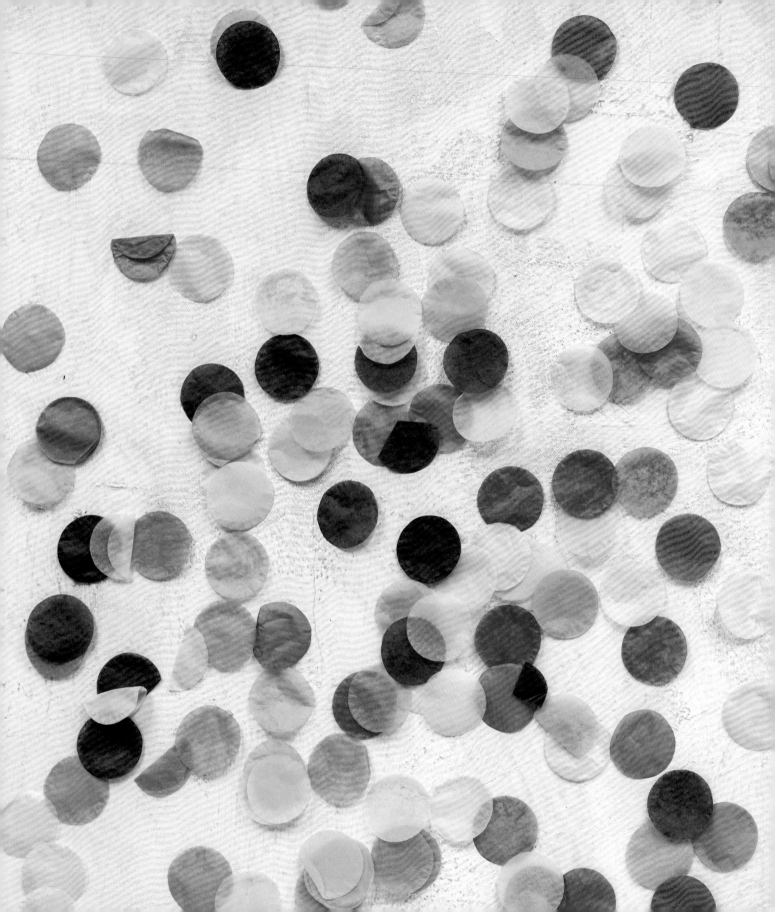

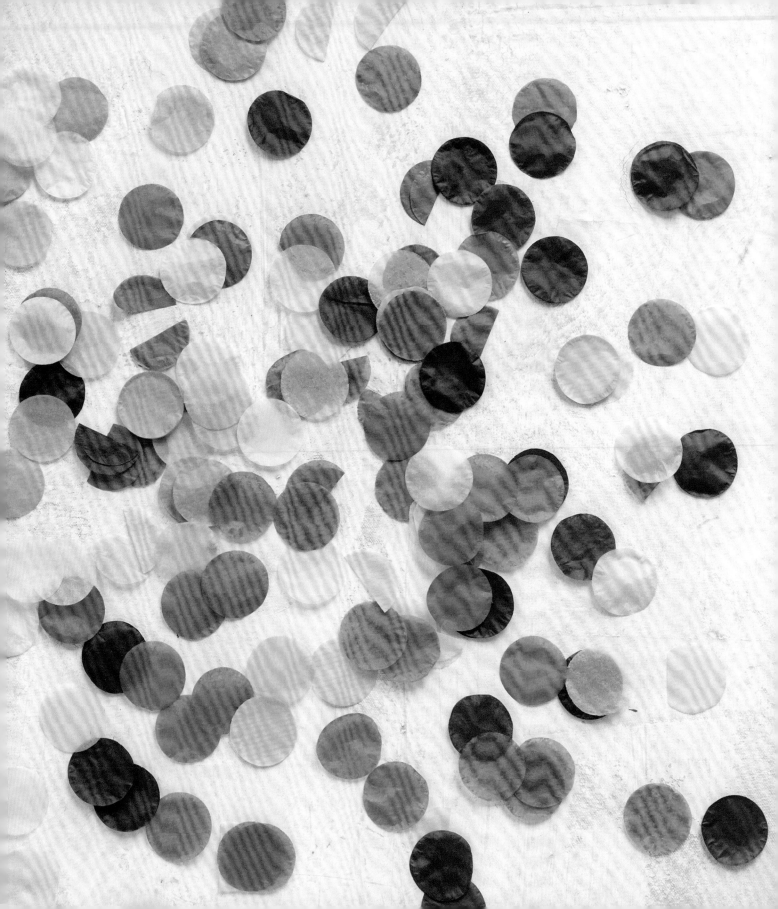

Editor: Shawna Mullen
Designers: Deb Wood, Heesang Lee
Production Manager: Katie Gaffney

Photography by Chaunté Vaughn
Tutorial photography by Anna Killian
Wardrobe styling by Aliza Wride
Creative direction and styling by
Brittany Watson Jepsen

Library of Congress Control Number:
2017944946

ISBN: 978-1-4197-2900-3
eISBN: 978-1-68335-215-0

Printed and bound in China
10 9 8 7 6 5 4 3 2 1

Abrams books are available at special
discounts when purchased in quantity for
premiums and promotions as well as fund-
raising or educational use. Special editions
can also be created to specification. For
details, contact specialsales@abramsbooks.
com or the address below.

ABRAMS The Art of Books
195 Broadway, New York, NY 10007
abramsbooks.com

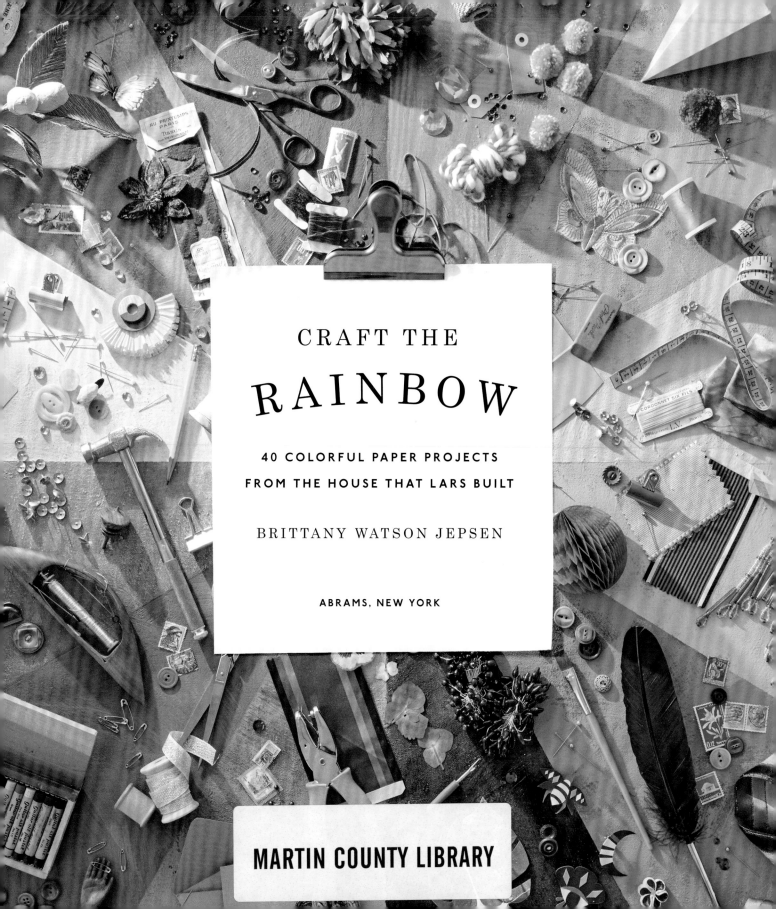

CRAFT THE
RAINBOW

40 COLORFUL PAPER PROJECTS
FROM THE HOUSE THAT LARS BUILT

BRITTANY WATSON JEPSEN

ABRAMS, NEW YORK

*"The purest and most
thoughtful minds
are those which love
color the most."*

—JOHN RUSKIN

Dedication

TO MY MOTHER
who taught me to
get down and messy.
Mess-makers unite!

TO PAUL
whose culinary skills
kept me alive during
the writing of this book

**TO MY GRANDMOTHER
DOROTHY**
whose legendary sewing
room continues to inspire

**TO THE
ORIGINAL LARS**
my dad, who gave me
all the tools I needed
to take a leap

Foreword by DARCY MILLER 11

INTRODUCTION 12

THE CRAFT CLOSET 14

BASIC FOLDING TECHNIQUES 18

EXPLORING COLOR 20

PINK 24

RED 36

ORANGE 50

YELLOW 62

GREEN 72

BLUE 84

PURPLE 94

WHITE 102

RAINBOW 116

TEMPLATES 164

RESOURCES 188

ACKNOWLEDGMENTS 190

FOREWORD

What's one thing we all feel passionately about? Color. Everyone from age two to ninety-two has an answer to the question, "What's your favorite color?" And that response changes as we do. Regardless of whether we realize it, we are constantly thinking about color—from how to paint our walls to what to wear, plant in our gardens, and apply to our lips. Color is such an important part of our lives and the source of so much inspiration and vivid memories.

Brittany Watson Jepsen's obsession with and attention to color is one of the reasons I became such a big fan of her style in the first place, avidly following her crafting genius on her must-read blog, *The House That Lars Built.* When Brittany asked me to write the foreword for this book, I was so honored. For me, choosing a color or colors is where I start when planning any celebration. Brittany brings this connection to another level entirely. Take one glance through the photos in this book and Brittany's creativity and sense of fun will come through, well, in living color.

In *Craft the Rainbow*, Brittany shares not only the instructive ways that color can be used, but also so many of her own stories about color. I love that all the inspiring projects are beautiful and carefully thought out, but also deeply personal and connected to Brittany's memories. And, of course, while reading this book, so many of my own vibrant memories came to mind, from the distinct varied colors of the teacups at my grandmother's house when I was a child, to the daisy party I threw for the first birthday of my oldest daughter, Daisy, at a picnic that was bursting with yellow and white.

As it travels through the spectrum, *Craft the Rainbow* guides readers through creating colorful crafts and memories—and ultimately makes mixing, matching, and making your own color stories less intimidating. From the rich cerulean blues of the cyanotypes to the saturated pop of orange in the Scandinavian-inspired garlands, the projects in *Craft the Rainbow* will show anyone who reads it a new way to look at your favorite hues. And I love that along with being inspired to think about these vibrant colors, we get the step-by-step instructions to make these beautiful projects.

As promised in the title, this book takes you on a journey not just over the rainbow, but through it. It's amazing to see how Brittany experiences color through the pages of *Craft the Rainbow,* but even more rewarding is the way this book will inspire you to tell your own color story, now and always.

Darcy Miller

—*Darcy Miller*
author, crafter, illustrator, and celebrations expert

I started the #CraftTheRainbow hashtag on a whim. I needed a photo to add to my Instagram feed for the day, so I looked around my studio, desperate for something quick to snap. I spotted a pile of crepe paper with a roll in every color of the rainbow. Bingo! That ought to do it. I spent some time arranging the rolls this way and that way before I finally realized that ordinary objects always look extraordinary when organized neatly—it's a not-so-scientific fact—so in rainbow order they went. I got so excited about my crafted rainbow that I announced, rashly, that I was going to post a new collection of craft materials in rainbow order every day for thirty days. I quickly posted to Instagram, and as fast as you can say "Me Lucky Charms," the people spoke. They loved it. I kept true to my promise, and readers joined in with their own crafted rainbows. Soon it was several thousand people, then tens of thousands of people. Turns out everyone loves rainbows!

Recognizing the allure of ROYGBP (red, orange, yellow, green, blue, purple), I set out to write a craft book that involved forty rainbow craft projects. However, over time the individual colors started to speak to me, and I felt compelled to tell their stories. Each one begged for more explanation. I began asking myself questions like, *What exactly do the colors of the rainbow mean? How and why do they affect us? How do we use them harmoniously with other colors? Why do certain colors look better with other colors than on their own?*

In interior design school, I gained an understanding of color theory and the psychology of color, but applying this to craft projects was a new challenge. How do you successfully pair colors to design a successful project? The more I explored, the more I was reminded of my personal relationships with colors. Color can trigger your emotions, memories, tastes, and desires, like drinking a big cup of nostalgia.

This book is a celebration of color, an ode to the natural phenomenon of the rainbow, and a festival of paper crafts all rolled into one. In it you'll find crafts in every shade, along with tips on how to harmoniously use colors in your own projects. Perhaps the stories I share with you will prompt connections to your own memories, and you'll realize why you surround yourself with certain hues. In that case, consider this a color intervention.

Craft the Rainbow is arranged to be an all-encompassing color experience. Flip through the rainbow of chapters—pink, red, orange, yellow, green, blue, purple, white—before arriving in color paradise: sixteen rainbow crafts for those of us who can't pick a favorite color. (Then, for a fun surprise, flip it backward for a secret, hypnotic message: You . . . will . . . make . . . every . . . project . . . in . . . this . . . book.) In addition, pay special attention to the quotes sprinkled throughout the book. I invited some of my favorite creatives to answer the question, "What's your favorite color?" Their answers are charmingly surprising, and they reveal a bit more than their public personae might suggest. Finally, each project is measured to the length of some of my favorite TV shows, movies, and podcasts. There is always a way to make time for your crafting, even if it's at the end of a long workday and all you want to do is watch the latest episode of *The Bachelor*. This book has a craft that fits perfectly in any time frame, or you can do it in stages according to your busy schedule.

I always knew I loved color and considered it one of the most defining elements of my work, but it wasn't until I put pen to paper (and made forty paper craft projects!) that I understood just how much color has influenced me. I hope this book encourages you to take your own creative color journey. And when it does, be sure to tag it with #CraftTheRainbow.

Brittany

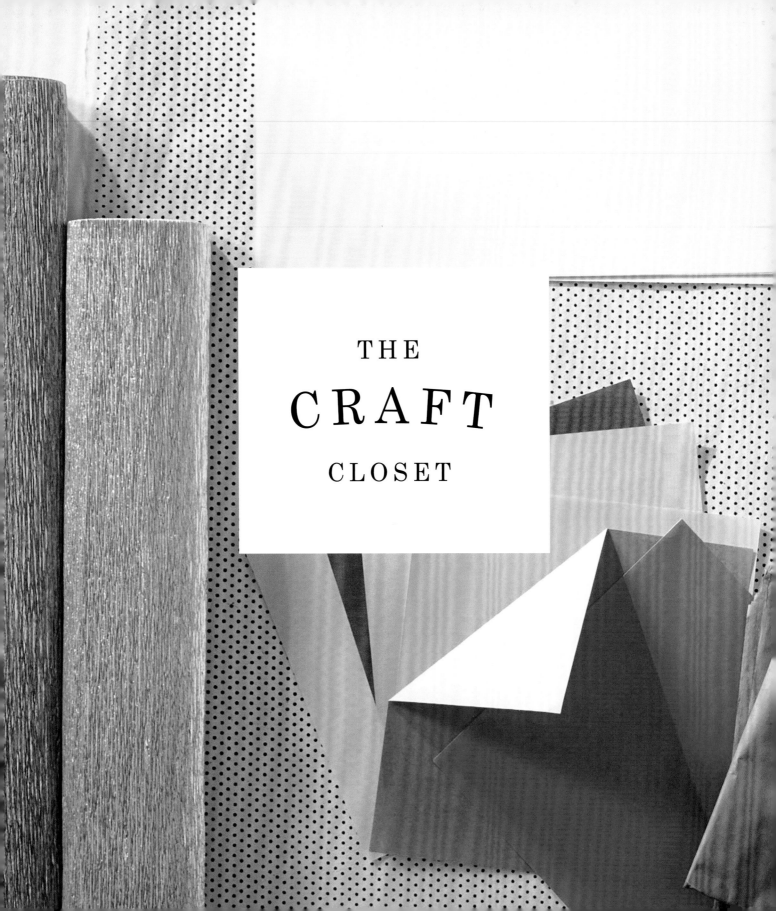

THE
CRAFT
CLOSET

PAPER

THE PROJECTS in this book are made from paper, my favorite crafting medium, along with a few other items. I use a variety of specialty paper types in addition to everyday papers from around the house, but you can use just one type of paper to make things simpler, easier, and faster—in fact, a good DIY project should always be one of those three things. I'm constantly surprised at the versatility and strength of paper. Here's the rundown:

NEWSPAPER

You may no longer subscribe to the print version, but newsprint is essential for crafting, especially papier-mâché and similar techniques.

WATERCOLOR PAPER

It's sturdy enough to hold up to wear and tear.

VINTAGE PAPERS

One of my hobbies is finding great vintage materials, from office papers to pretty decorative prints.

POSTER BOARD

Buy this in packs of ten to save money.

CREPE PAPER ROLLS

My guilty pleasure. This book calls for a variety of weights, all of which achieve different effects.

TISSUE PAPER

Perfect for gift-wrapping or more delicate crafting. It comes in a wide spectrum of colors.

BUTCHER PAPER

You can buy this on the cheap at a party store by the foot or in bulk.

PASTEL PAPER

Pastel refers not to color, but type. It's a bit more expensive, but for the right occasion it also feels more luxurious.

ORIGAMI PAPER

Buy the rainbow packs for the best selection of colors.

CARDSTOCK

Limitless colors and great for everyday crafting.

SCRAPBOOK PAPER

Lighter than cardstock. It's perfect for most crafting and comes in fun textures.

CREPE PAPER STREAMERS

Get these at the dollar store.

LEGAL PAD

You probably already have one lying around.

PRINTER PAPER

You likely have this too. The cheap stuff is all you need.

CUPCAKE LINERS

You can use parchment, glassine, or foil in an assortment of colors. Get creative.

PAINT CHIPS

The price is right, and they come in beautiful colors.

PAPER SCRAPS

Save them all!

SEAMLESS PHOTOGRAPHY PAPER

My secret weapon when I need good-quality bulk paper.

TOOLS & SUPPLIES

EACH PROJECT includes a list of materials you will need, but keep your craft closet stocked with these basic craft supplies. Of course, you can also get pretty far on your creative color journey with just paper, scissors, and an inexpensive glue gun.

1 PAINT

All kinds. The projects in this book use acrylics, watercolor, gouache, and even samples of house paint. (House paint is my favorite trick. Just go to the home-improvement store and ask for a sample of any color. It costs about the same as a tube of acrylic, and you get a lot more for your money. Plus you can have the store customize it to make any color you want.)

2 BONE FOLDER

For making crisp folds and creases.

3 SCISSORS

A good pair will take you far.

4 SEWING KIT

Only basic sewing skills are required for these projects.

5 ADHESIVES

Glue gun (my best friend), glue stick, and basic white glue.

6 TAPES

Duct, painter's, washi, double-sided, and masking all come in handy.

7 PAINTBRUSHES

Keep on hand a variety of sizes and points, especially foam crafting brushes.

8 PENCIL AND ERASER

This doesn't have to be fancy.

9 RULER

A metal one with a cork backing is best.

10 MEASURING TAPE

Simple and cheap is fine.

11 FOAM RISERS

These give a little lift to papers that appear too flat (not shown).

12 FRINGE SCISSORS

You'll find plenty of ways to use these, from making piñatas to texturizing.

13 CRAFT BLADE AND CUTTING MAT

Get extra blades, and swap in a fresh one when the cuts become less crisp.

14 PUNCHES

These projects use the basic forms, like circle and square.

15 WIRE AND WIRE CUTTERS

Get floral wire in a variety of thicknesses, and cutters to snip.

16 CRAFT CUTTER

This is my new favorite. There are so many wonderful SVG files, or images formatted to be cut using a craft cutter (not shown).

17 CLAMPS

Always helpful for securing items together.

18 STICKY TACK

Surprisingly strong and it won't damage surfaces.

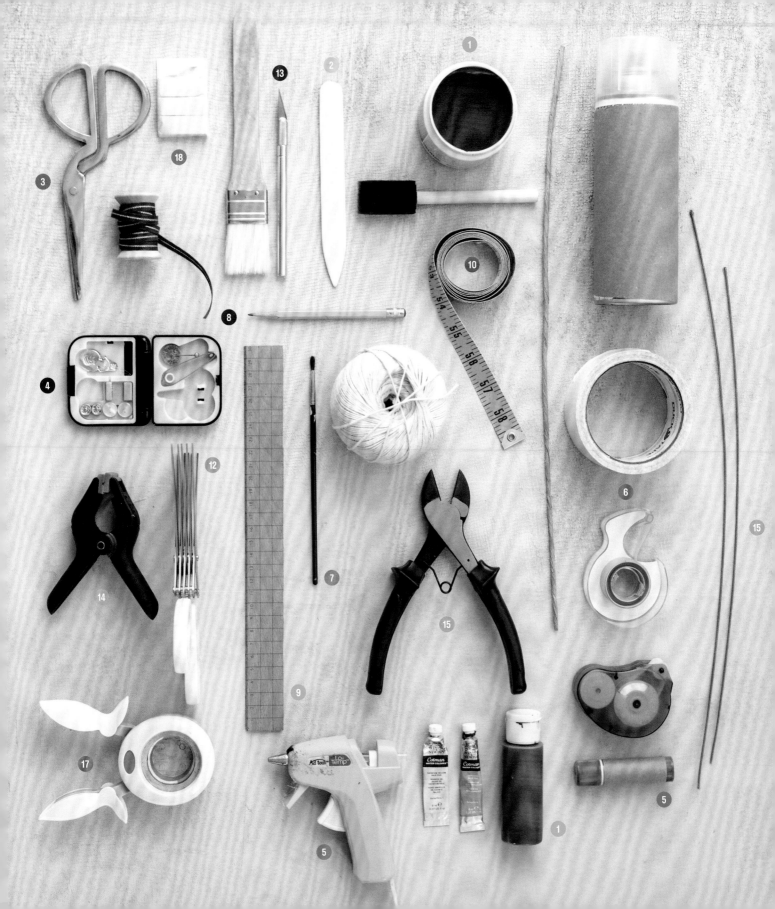

BASIC

FOLDING

TECHNIQUES

SEVERAL PROJECTS

in this book teach you how to create specific folding projects. These three basic folds will assist you:

Ⓐ VALLEY FOLD

With the right (blue) side up, fold in half diagonally so the right sides touch. When unfolded with the right side (blue) side up, the crease will form a valley.

Ⓑ MOUNTAIN FOLD

With the wrong (white) side up, fold in half diagonally so the wrong sides touch. When unfolded with the right (blue) side up, the crease will form a mountain.

Ⓒ FORMING SHAPES

After you have made the creases according to the mountain or valley designations, lay the paper flat. It will start to form the desired shape along the creases. Use your hands to further push in the valley folds and pop out the mountain folds. When you have sharpened all the folds, you should be able to fold the entire paper accordingly.

Ⓓ UNIVERSAL FOLD

This is created by folding your paper both ways, Mountain and Valley, along the same crease.

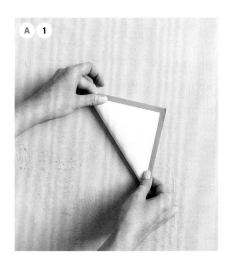

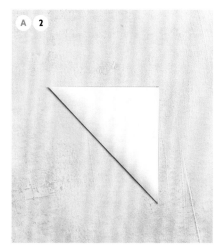

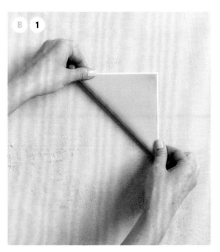

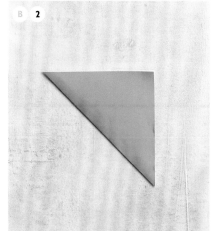

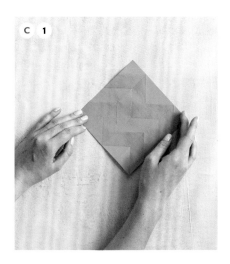

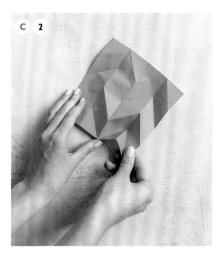

EXPLORING
COLOR

COLOR THEORY

THE COLOR WHEEL is made up of the three main primary colors that cannot be made from any other colors—red, yellow, and blue. Secondary colors—orange, green, and purple—are created from mixing two primary colors: red + yellow = orange; red + blue = purple; blue + yellow = green. Tertiary colors are created by mixing one primary and one secondary color. They include blue-green, yellow-green, yellow-orange, red-orange, red-purple, and blue-purple. Knowing these terms will help you speak the language of color more fluently.

ANALOGOUS COLORS

Three colors in a row on a full color wheel, such as red, red-orange, orange.

COMPLEMENTARY COLORS

Colors that sit opposite one another on the color wheel, like blue and orange or purple and yellow.

HUE

That property of a color identifying a specific, named wavelength of light, such as green, red, purple. This is the true color without tint or shade. This is generally what we mean when we say *color*.

SHADE

Hues darkened with black.

TINT

Hues lightened with white (aka pastels).

TONE

A pure hue with gray added.

VALUE

The indicator of how light or dark a color is.

WARM COLORS

Colors whose relative visual temperature makes them seem warm, like red-purple, red, red-orange, orange, yellow-orange, and yellow.

COOL COLORS

Colors whose relative visual temperature makes them seem cool, including green, blue-green, blue, blue-purple, and purple.

NEUTRAL COLORS

Colors not associated with any single hue, like blacks, whites, grays, and dull gray-browns. You can create a neutral by mixing complementary hues.

SATURATION

The intensity of a color. A color with high saturation is devoid of gray; a color low in saturation is closer to gray.

COLOR STORIES

ALTHOUGH THIS BOOK leads you through each color of the rainbow and examines why certain colors work well together, it is my personal take on color selection—my color story, if you will. All my experiences and surroundings have informed my color choices, just as your experiences have informed your color stories (although you may not yet recognize it). Make a note of what catches your eye. Take pictures. Collect postcards, fabric samples, paint swatches—whatever strikes your fancy. You'll begin to recognize that you gravitate to certain colors. Start describing why you like them, using the terms listed in the previous section. Once you articulate your preferences, you will be better equipped to understand why you like something and what you should do with it.

A helpful exercise is to gather your favorite colors around you and start pairing them. You might find that they blend well naturally. If they aren't a good mix, use your color theory knowledge to make it work. Perhaps you need to tone (add gray to) a red hue so it's more harmonious to live with. Or perhaps you need to add white (tint) so it becomes a beautiful pink shade. This is the fun part! Start evaluating your favorite colors and figure out how they can work to your benefit. Here's my personal color board.

Mountain Laurel (Kalmia latifolia) State Flower of Connecticut

A Hedge of Roses, California.

FIRST OF ALL, YOU'RE REALLY PRETTY

A Field of California Poppies.

NOTEBO

gør mere af det der gør dig glad

"**PINK** gives balance to my work, and I love pairing it against cooler colors and neutrals like browns and grays."

—LISA CONGDON, *artist and illustrator*

When I was growing up, I did not love **PINK**. *Hot* **PINK** *was used to sell princess toys to little girls like me. I was no tomboy, but even at a young age I had my reservations about such an in-your-face color. Over the years I've come to see it as a well-rounded neutral with which you can pair most colors of the rainbow.* **PINK** *immediately softens or freshens any look. I humbly declare today's blush* **PINK** *to be what beige was in the 1980s (aka everywhere!), but I hope history will be a bit kinder to it.* **PINK** *is such an easy, exquisite solution. It is my secret weapon.*

FUN FACTS ABOUT PINK:

→ NOT EVEN A CENTURY AGO, **PINK** WAS LINKED TO LITTLE BOYS, NOT LITTLE GIRLS. → THE TERM **PINK** COMES FROM GARDEN PINK, A SMALL, SWEET-SMELLING FLOWER. → PRINCESS DIANA NICKNAMED BRITISH POUND NOTES AFTER THEIR COLORS; SHE CALLED FIFTY-POUND NOTES "**PINK** GRANNIES."

OVERSIZE MAGNOLIA

I realized my wedding was probably going to be my only opportunity to throw the biggest party of my life, so it had to be absolutely magical! With the help of some willing victims—my mom and my sister—we got to work concocting dozens of oversize paper flowers for the centerpieces and a single watercolor poppy for my bouquet.

This oversize magnolia is another take on my bridal bouquet. It would be lovely for a bridesmaid bouquet, too. It's surprisingly simple to assemble, and unlike fresh flowers, you can hold on to it forever (but keep it away from dogs and clumsy hands). After the event, store it in a vase or make it part of a mantel display.

HOW TO USE PINK

One way to elevate a project and keep it from looking too craft-y or homemade (yes, that can take on a negative connotation) is to keep the palette simple and work with the strength of a single color. There is power in a one-color exploration! I chose monochromatic pinks to blend with the selection of bridesmaid dresses and bring out the different shades within the pink family. Using watercolor paints allowed further experimentation with transparency and layers. Consider your wedding colors when selecting your own palette.

COLORS

monochromatic pinks

TIME

an afternoon listening to your wedding playlist with the bridal party

INSPIRATION

my wedding bouquet

(MATERIALS)

templates (page 166)

scissors

1 pad of 9 by 12-inch (23 by 30.5-cm) watercolor paper, 5 to 6 sheets per flower

pencil

fringe scissors

2 to 3 sheets of 12 by 12-inch (30.5 by 30.5-cm) green cardstock

bone folder

watercolor set with paintbrush

180-gram dark green crepe paper roll

18-inch (46-cm) 18-gauge floral wires (one per flower; they come in a pack of 20)

glue gun

hole punch

1½ by 12-inch (4 by 30.5-cm) wooden dowel (optional)

pale pink ribbon

fringe scissors

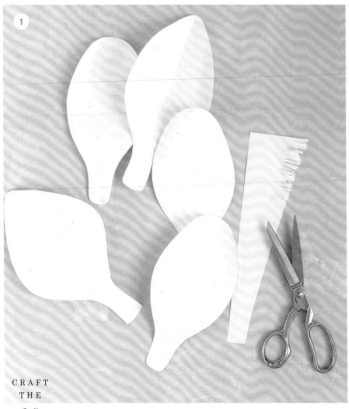

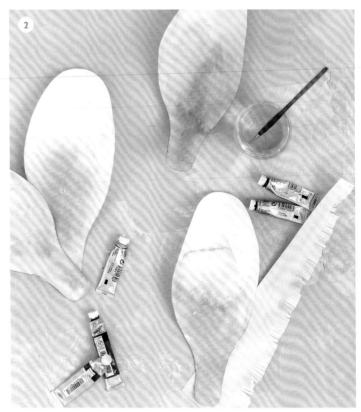

(INSTRUCTIONS)

1 Copy the templates onto watercolor paper, and cut out. Trace seven narrow petals, three wider petals, and one stamen onto watercolor paper, and cut out. Fringe the edge of the stamen by making narrowly spaced cuts up one side. Trace leaves (you will need 1 to 2 per flower) onto green card-stock, and cut out. Score the middle of each leaf with a bone folder.

2 Paint each petal on both sides with pink and purple watercolors, leaving the tip white and gradually getting darker toward the base. Paint the stamen with yellow and green watercolors. Let dry. Curl the stamen and the edges of each petal around a pencil or a paintbrush handle.

3 Cut a long ½-inch-wide (1.3-cm) strip of green crepe paper against the grain. Stretch it out. (Be gentle! It can tear easily.) Glue at the top of a wire. Wrap the crepe paper around to the end of the wire, and secure with glue.

4 Tightly roll the fringed stamen into a cylinder.

5 Punch a hole into the bottom of each petal and layer them onto the wire underneath the stamen. Insert the top of a paper-wrapped wire into the stamen and adhere with glue. Continue until you have a full flower blooming around the stamen. Glue a leaf or two to the base of the flower. (If you want a more solid stem, wrap a wooden dowel with green crepe paper, securing with glue at both ends, and then carefully wind the wire around the dowel.) Cut a length of pink ribbon and tie a bow to the stem, underneath the leaves.

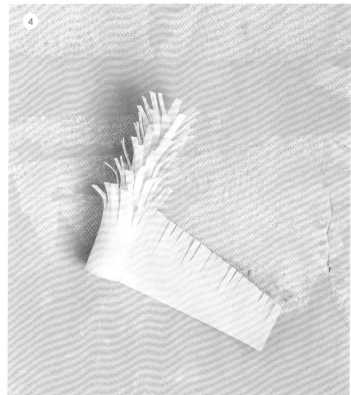

FLORAL WREATH COLLAGE

love the way that collage works with materials you already have or can get easily and cheaply. I found loads of botanical books and magazines at a thrift shop, as well as flower catalogs, and spent an evening watching movies and cutting out flowers. Or you can invite some friends over for a crafternoon.

HOW TO USE PINK

One of my favorite color combinations is a happy lemon yellow combined with the softness of a blush or even a bright fuchsia (see my yellow-and-pink website). I welcomed all shades of pink and yellow here to create depth of color. The antiqued yellow pages add another grounding patina.

COLORS

pink and yellow

TIME

an afternoon watching
North and South

INSPIRATION

classic floral wreath

(MATERIALS)

old botanical books, gardening magazines, flower catalogs

standard scissors and small, sharp scissors

cardstock

adhesive spray or glue stick

flat wooden wreath base

glue gun

foam sticker squares

(INSTRUCTIONS)

1   Cut out flowers from books, magazines, and catalogs.

2   Paste the flowers onto cardstock with adhesive spray or a glue stick to make them stiffer. Let dry.

3   Cut carefully around each flower with small, sharp scissors, as close to the edge as possible. Use a trash bag to dispose of scraps as you go.

4   Arrange a bottom layer of flowers on the wreath base and use the glue gun to affix. Save the real showstoppers for the top. Once the bottom layer is complete, use foam sticker squares to create second and third layers around the wreath.

OPTIONAL:

✳ *Top with a beautiful ribbon or a faux bird—or both!*

PAPER WEAVING TECHNIQUE

Designing projects might be my favorite part of crafting, and it has definitely been one of my favorite parts of creating this book. One way you might want to brainstorm potential projects is by applying a traditional craft to paper. This is challenging, which keeps it exciting, but it doesn't take a toll on the bank account. Score! These paper weavings are a perfect example. The idea of acquiring a loom, yarns, and, most important, patience—all needed for real fiber weaving—exhausts me. Weaving with paper is much easier. You might spend a chunk of time cutting out strips, but after that it's fun to come up with creative designs.

HOW TO USE PINK

I chose a pink and gray-blue scheme. Weaving lends itself to using a variety of colors, but as with the magnolias, I limited the color palette to keep the weavings cohesive, but here's your chance to have a great time selecting all your favorite colors.

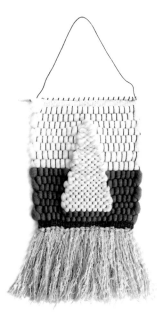

(MATERIALS)

sketch pad paper

acrylic paint

paintbrush

paper cutter or scissors

masking tape

spray adhesive

12 by 12-inch (30.5 by 30.5-cm) or 11 by 17-inch (28 by 43-cm) pieces of cardstock

COLORS

pinks and blues

TIME

a lazy weekend listening to Tina Fey's *Bossypants*

INSPIRATION

traditional fiber weaving

1. Paint your paper in various shades of pinks, blues, and grays. I also texturized mine with stripes, dots, and splatters to give the weaving more life. Without paint, the look is more flat, which is fine too. Let dry. Cut the paper into ¼-inch-wide (6-mm) strips.

2. Lay out the first layer of vertical strips very close together.

3. Apply a piece of masking tape to the top of the strips to hold them in place. Weave another layer of strips horizontally over and under the vertical strips as desired.

4. Once the pattern is complete, use spray adhesive to affix the weaving to a piece of cardstock. Trim so you have a clean edge all the way around. Frame the weaving as an art piece, hang it like a wreath on the door, or use as a table runner or backdrop under small collections.

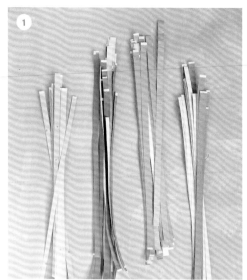

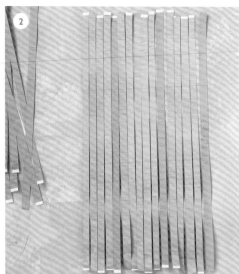

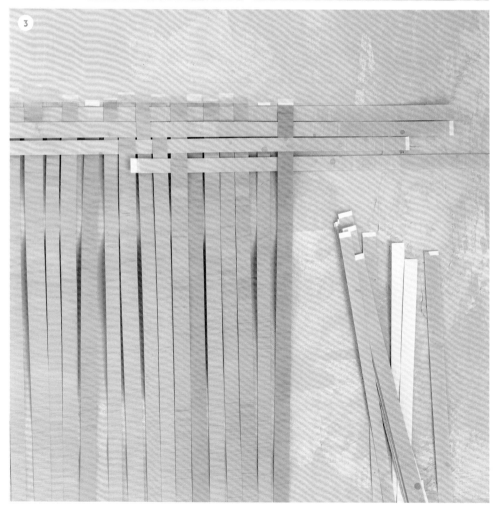

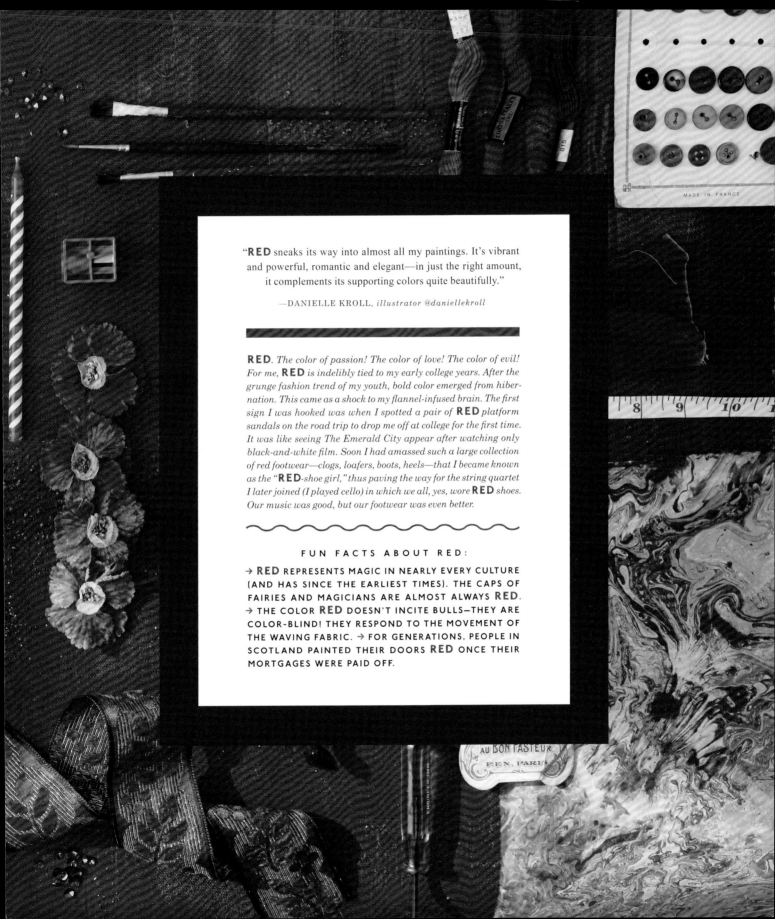

"**RED** sneaks its way into almost all my paintings. It's vibrant and powerful, romantic and elegant—in just the right amount, it complements its supporting colors quite beautifully."

—DANIELLE KROLL, *illustrator @daniellekroll*

RED. *The color of passion! The color of love! The color of evil! For me,* **RED** *is indelibly tied to my early college years. After the grunge fashion trend of my youth, bold color emerged from hibernation. This came as a shock to my flannel-infused brain. The first sign I was hooked was when I spotted a pair of* **RED** *platform sandals on the road trip to drop me off at college for the first time. It was like seeing The Emerald City appear after watching only black-and-white film. Soon I had amassed such a large collection of red footwear—clogs, loafers, boots, heels—that I became known as the "*RED*-shoe girl," thus paving the way for the string quartet I later joined (I played cello) in which we all, yes, wore* **RED** *shoes. Our music was good, but our footwear was even better.*

FUN FACTS ABOUT RED:

→ **RED** REPRESENTS MAGIC IN NEARLY EVERY CULTURE (AND HAS SINCE THE EARLIEST TIMES). THE CAPS OF FAIRIES AND MAGICIANS ARE ALMOST ALWAYS **RED**. → THE COLOR **RED** DOESN'T INCITE BULLS—THEY ARE COLOR-BLIND! THEY RESPOND TO THE MOVEMENT OF THE WAVING FABRIC. → FOR GENERATIONS, PEOPLE IN SCOTLAND PAINTED THEIR DOORS **RED** ONCE THEIR MORTGAGES WERE PAID OFF.

DALA HORSE PIÑATA

When I was young, I discovered the work of the Swedish artist Carl Larsson in a book from my local library. I was instantly drawn to his charming portrayal of childhood and twinkling Swedish meadows. I longed to be a part of that folk-infused, color-permeated world. You can imagine the sense of awe I felt when I attended a field trip to the Swedish countryside to visit Larsson's Sundborn home while studying in Copenhagen, Denmark. On the bus ride we made a stop at the world's largest Dala horse, which is traditionally a small wood-carved statuette that represents Sweden. The enormity of the statue, about twenty-two feet (6.5 m) tall, inspired this piñata version, which would be a fun décor piece or entertainment at your next party. Fill it with old-school candies as a nod to the past.

HOW TO USE RED

When brainstorming projects for this chapter, traditional red symbols came to mind immediately: stop signs, caution signs, national flags. Many of them represent authority and can be a bit intimidating. My challenge was to use red in a lovely way. I softened up the red-and-white palette by imagining it in the context of a Swedish meadow. I added green foliage (see the how-to in Orange Swedish Garlands, page 53) and some florals (see Ikebana Floral Arrangement, page 121) for extra finesse. Consider adding elements from nature when you want to soften something.

COLORS

red and white

TIME

watching the new *Pride and Prejudice*

INSPIRATION

traditional Swedish Dala horses

(MATERIALS)

templates (page 168)

white paper

scissors

pencil

2 to 3 large pieces of cardboard (2 by 3 feet / 61 by 91 cm)

craft knife

masking or duct tape

hole punch

thin rope for hanging, at least 10 feet (3 m) or enough for desired location

red tissue paper

fringe scissors

glue gun

white cardstock

spray adhesive

(INSTRUCTIONS)

1 Copy the templates onto white paper, and cut out. Trace the horse twice onto cardboard, and cut out with a craft knife. If there are folds in your cardboard, strengthen them with tape to prevent bending (not shown).

2 Using a craft knife or scissors, cut strips of cardboard as wide as you want your horse to be. I cut mine 4 inches (10 cm) wide against the grain of the cardboard (in the opposite direction of the lines) to make the cardboard more malleable. Loosen the strips by rolling them gently so the cardboard is easier to bend.

3 Tape the strips to the edge of a horse cutout, bending and securing at intervals so the strip lies smooth against the horse. You will need multiple strips to go around the whole horse. When one strip ends, begin where you left off. Do not leave any gaps.

4 When you have affixed cardboard strips around the entire horse, punch a hole at the top. Place the other horse cutout on top of the cutout with the taped sides, and secure with tape. Use a craft knife to cut a U-shaped hole at the back of the horse. This is the flap through which you will insert candy.

5 Cut strips of tissue paper 1½ to 2 inches (4 to 5 cm) wide. Fold into layers. Fringe the edge by making narrowly spaced cuts on one side, leaving about ½ inch (1.3 cm) unfringed.

6 Beginning at the bottom, use the glue gun to affix the tissue-paper strips onto the horse, overlapping the strips to give the horse a fluffy appearance. Continue until you've covered the entire horse.

7 Trace the remaining template pieces onto white cardstock, and cut out. Use spray adhesive to glue the saddle, mane, and bridle onto the tissue-covered horse. Add a floral collar, if desired, following Ikebana Floral Arrangement on page 120 and the Orange Swedish Garlands on page 52. Punch two holes at the neck of the horse (not shown). This is where you will thread your piñata for hanging at the end. Fill the Dala horse with candy, and hang from a tree or the ceiling.

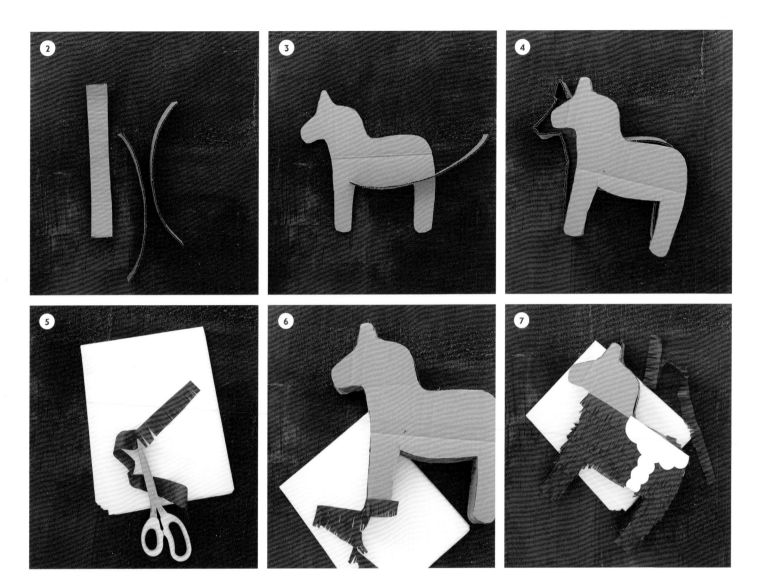

CLEOPATRA

KING HENRY

QUEEN MARGRETHE

KING TITAN

DRINKING STRAW PARTY CROWNS

f you're like me, you find yourself fascinated by the clean lines, simplified shapes, and primary colors of modern design. I liked the Bauhaus school of thought so much, I studied it—and wrote my final paper about the infamous parties. The school's mission was to bring together arts and crafts, and the parties were its pinnacle. The graphics department composed beautiful posters to announce the events, while the costume department designed the most stunning (albeit slightly jarring) costumes for the dance department, which choreographed new ballets—and so on. What I would give to have attended a Bauhaus party!

These paper drinking straw hats are my ode to the Bauhaus parties, complete with their signature color palette and graphic shapes. They're perfect for birthday parties or dress-up.

HOW TO USE RED

Red, yellow, and blue are the basic building blocks of the color wheel. They are often used in a juvenile setting, but they are sophisticated enough for an adult crowd—if you darken the hues slightly. Cranberry is substituted for the pure red, mustard replaces bright yellow, and cerulean blue takes over for ultramarine. You can also keep the colors bright for a child's party.

(MATERIALS)

red construction paper

scissors

packs of paper drinking straws in reds, yellows, and blues

glue gun

craft knife

bag of ¼-inch (6-mm) red or yellow pom-poms (optional)

COLORS

red, yellow, blue

TIME

an episode or two of *30 Rock*

INSPIRATION

traditional crowns

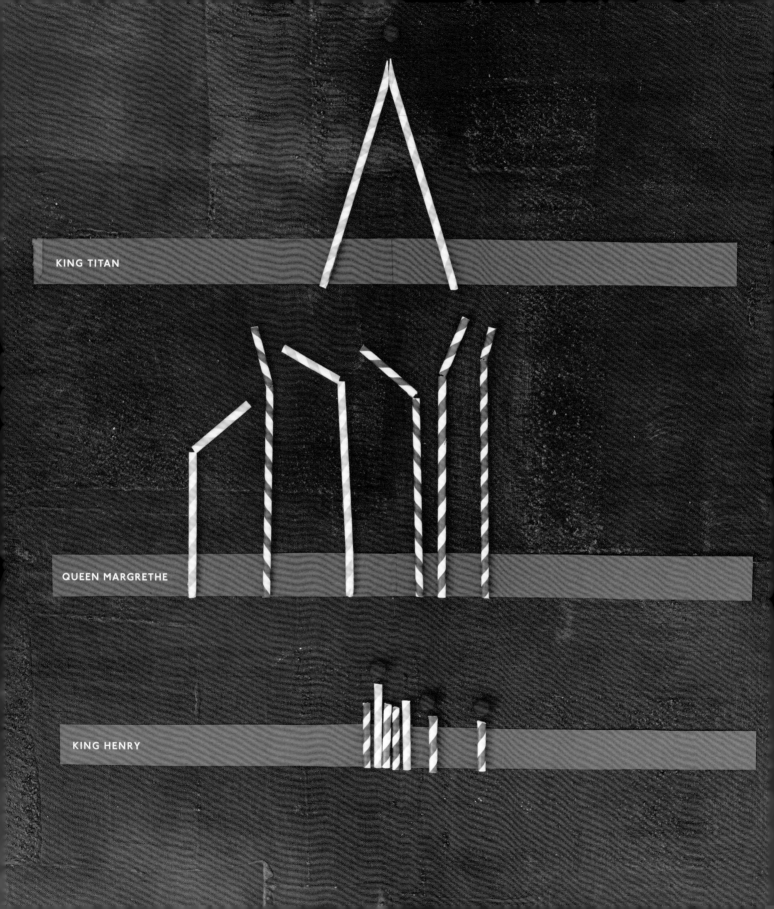

KING TITAN

QUEEN MARGRETHE

KING HENRY

CLEOPATRA

1 Cut a 1-inch-wide (2.5-cm) piece of construction paper into a headband large enough to wrap around the wearer's head. Leave 1 inch (2.5 cm) of overlap.

2 Cut a point on one of the straws. Place the straw in the center of the band, and glue in place.

3 With a craft knife, make a small diagonal cut ½ inch (1.3 cm) from the top of 20 straws. Place the straws at varying heights on the head-band. Glue them in place, working outward from the center straw. Make sure all the diagonals on each respective side face the same way. Cut off any excess straw at the bottom to create a nice finished edge. Glue the ends of the headband together.

KING HENRY

1 Cut a 1-inch-wide (2.5-cm) piece of construction paper into a headband large enough to wrap around the wearer's head. Leave 1 inch (2.5 cm) of overlap.

2 Cut straw pieces to varying heights—anywhere from 1½ to 3½ inches (4 to 9 cm). You will need enough straw pieces to cover the width of the crown. Glue straw pieces onto the headband.

3 Cut off any excess straw at the bottom to create a nice finished edge. Glue the ends of the headband together. Optional: Glue pom-poms to the top for an extra flourish.

QUEEN MARGRETHE

1 Cut a 1-inch-wide (2.5-cm) piece of construction paper into a headband large enough to wrap around the wearer's head. Leave 1 inch (2.5 cm) of overlap.

2 With a craft knife, cut a small slit in 40 to 50 straws anywhere from ½ inch to 4 inches (1.3 to 10 cm) from the top and bend them slightly (A). Place the straws at varying heights on the headband.

3 Glue them in place, working outward from the center straw. Cut off any excess straw at the bottom to create a nice finished edge. Glue the ends of the headband together.

KING TITAN

1 Cut a 1-inch-wide (2.5-cm) piece of construction paper into a headband large enough to wrap around the wearer's head. Leave 1 inch (2.5 cm) of overlap.

2 With a craft knife, cut two straws diagonally from about ½ inch (1.3 cm) to the tip of the straw. Glue the straws together so they form a mountain peak (B).

3 Repeat this two more times, then glue all straws to the headband. Glue the ends of the headband together. Optional: Add pom-poms, if desired.

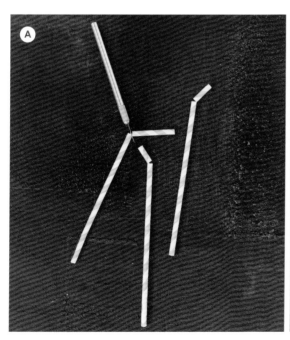

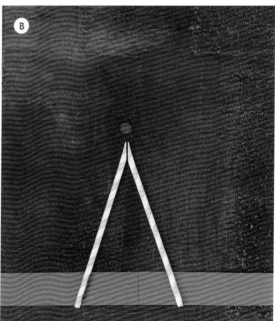

GEMSTONE FOLDED PAPER LAMP

Have you ever picked up a magazine just to kill some time in the airport or grocery store, only to find yourself completely immersed in the beautiful images? I stocked up on design magazines while I was waiting in the underground section of a train station in Cologne, Germany, on my way to visit friends in Paris. I had plenty of work to do, but instead I alternated between gazing out the train window and devouring my magazines. My eyes stopped on a stunning architectural table lamp made of beautiful wood veneer with angled geometric facets. The precision of the cuts required to make it was truly mind-blowing, as was the price tag.

This one isn't made of wood, but with just a plain piece of paper you can create simple folds to produce an impressive multifaceted gemstone table lamp. Just fold and wrap!

HOW TO USE RED

Red has the uncanny ability to suggest various moods, depending on the shade. Red-orange feels springy and fun, while red-violet feels more serious. This deep burgundy has a sophisticated air, especially when accented with a shiny gold and various other shades of red as accents.

COLORS

deep red and metallic gold

TIME

listening to Yo-Yo Ma's *Bach Suites*

INSPIRATION

gemstones

(MATERIALS)

template (page 169)

pastel paper (Canson Mi-Teintes has great colors in a perfect weight)

scissors

bone folder

glue gun

lamp base (this one is from Ikea)

binder clips

craft knife

metal ruler with grip

lampshade (found at a thrift store)

1A   1B   1C

(INSTRUCTIONS)

1   Copy the template onto the wrong side of the pastel paper (shown in white here, like the template), and cut out, making the height a little too long. (You can trim it to the perfect size after you have made all your folds and placed it over the lamp base.) Make universal folds (crease each fold in a mountain and a valley direction; see page 19) along the vertical lines of the template: Fold your paper in half vertically (A). Open the paper, and fold each of the halves in half (B). Open the paper again, and then continue to fold each half in half until you have made the appropriate number of creases (C). When you've made all the creases, lay the paper flat with the template side up. Make sure all the creases are folded according to the template. Accordion fold the entire sheet into something that is about 1 inch (2.5 cm) wide.

2   Using a bone folder, make additional folds according to the template. Thin papers fold more easily, but the folds are more fragile and collapse much more easily. Thick papers are difficult to crease, but they are much more durable and provide more structure. No matter what your paper thickness, make sure to crease each fold as sharply as you can. For thick papers, you might want to score your folds, but keep in mind that the scored side of the paper will create a valley fold.

3   Open the paper without unfolding any of the creases. Overlap the two outside edges so the folds of the first two and last two vertical segments align. Glue these overlapped edges together. Place the cylinder over the lamp base. Close up the base by pushing the valley folds in at the bottom and gluing them closed. Secure with binder clips until glue sets.

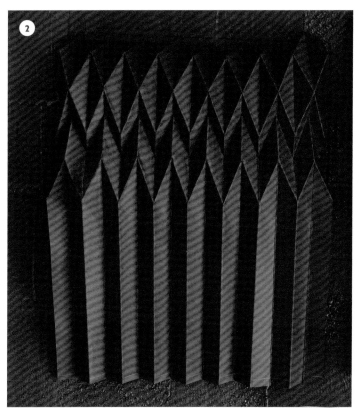

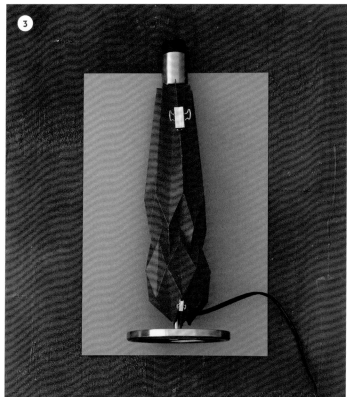

4 If your lamp cover is too tall, use a craft knife and metal ruler to trim it to size. Close the top by pinching the mountain folds and gluing them closed. Add the lamp-shade.

"I have a soft spot for **ORANGE**. It's slightly intellectual (a smarter variation of red than pink), and it pairs so well with navy and gray."

—KATIE HATCH, *creative director of Sleepy Jones*

*Despite often being associated with signs of alarm, **ORANGE** represents optimism and warmth. Think freshly squeezed **ORANGE** juice, monarch butterflies, cozy fires, plump persimmons, and sunsets.*

Author Kassia St. Clair reports the Impressionists first mastered the color, most notably when Claude Monet (my personal color hero) introduced the painting that changed the landscape (pun intended) of painting forever. Impression, Sunrise, *the work that named the movement, features a dripping bright **ORANGE** sun surrounded by a calm complementary blue, a device used by many other artists, including Gauguin and Van Gogh.*

FUN FACTS ABOUT ORANGE:

→ WHICH CAME FIRST, THE CHICKEN OR THE EGG? IN THIS CASE, IT WAS THE FRUIT! THE COLOR IS NAMED AFTER THE CITRUS. → LEGEND HAS IT THAT PRIOR TO THE SEVENTEENTH CENTURY, CARROTS WERE WHITE AND PURPLE UNTIL DUTCH GROWERS CULTIVATED **ORANGE** CARROTS AS A TRIBUTE TO WILLIAM OF **ORANGE**. → HERMÈS, THE LUXURY FASHION HOUSE, STARTED USING **ORANGE** PACKAGING BECAUSE OF A CARDBOARD SHORTAGE OF ITS SIGNATURE CREAM COLOR DURING THE SECOND WORLD WAR.

ORANGE SWEDISH GARLANDS

Can you trace your love of something to a certain person? I attribute my love of Scandinavia largely to my great-grandmother Marilla Zatelle (she made us promise that none of her progeny would name our kids after her—not to worry, Zatelle!). She kept an eight-inch-thick family history book that transported me to my Scandinavian roots. She also gave me a Swedish doll that came with a book describing several Swedish traditions, including the use of oranges as decorations at Christmastime. This paper orange garland is my ode to the custom. Bonus: You can reuse it year after year.

HOW TO USE ORANGE

If you are unsure of how to use a color, think about where you see the hue in nature and emulate that. (Nature makes it work every time.) While I may not like bright orange on its own, I love it on an orange tree because of the deep greens of the foliage and the natural wood branches. Suddenly, orange becomes sophisticated, rich, and beautiful.

COLORS

orange and green

TIME

listening to a retro Christmas playlist

INSPIRATION

oranges

(MATERIALS)

templates (page 170)

white paper

scissors

pencil

10 to 15 pieces of deep green cardstock

160- to 180-gram weight crepe paper rolls in various shades of dark green and orange

craft knife

glue gun

80 18-inch (46-cm) 22-gauge floral wires

2-inch (5-cm) Styrofoam balls, 18 total (or enough to spread across your mantel)

wire cutters

acrylic paint in oranges and corals (optional)

paintbrush (optional)

brown painter's paper

masking tape

(INSTRUCTIONS)

LEAVES

1 Copy the templates onto white paper, and cut out. Trace small leaves onto cardstock, and cut out. Trace larger leaves onto green crepe paper and cardstock, and cut out. Score the cardstock leaves down the middle with a craft knife.

2 To create small leaf boughs, glue small leaves onto floral wire. Leave a few inches of wire uncovered on both ends. I made about 25 small leaf boughs.

3 To create large leaf boughs, glue crepe paper leaves alternating with cardstock leaves onto floral wire. Leave a few inches of wire uncovered on both ends. I made about 35 large leaf boughs.

4 Wrap the small leaf boughs around the larger boughs. Twist the uncovered ends together.

ORANGES

5 Cut 5-inch-long (13 cm) strips of orange crepe paper along the grain. You'll need one strip for each orange. I made about 18 oranges. Twist the center of each strip 360 degrees.

6 Place a Styrofoam ball in the center of a twisted crepe paper strip. Pull and stretch the crepe paper tightly around the ball to cover completely.

7 Twist the crepe paper at the top of the ball, and secure with wire. Trim excess paper. Trim wire, leaving about 1 inch (2.5 cm). Paint details on the oranges, if desired, and glue a small leaf to cover the extra 1 inch (2.5 cm) of wire.

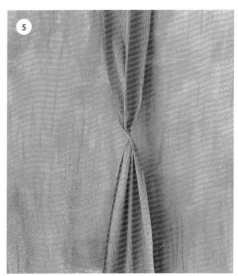

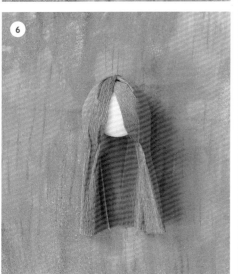

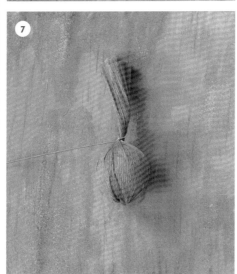

GARLAND

8 Measure the painter's paper to the length of your mantel. Consider how much swag you want to add and how much excess you'd like on both ends, and add a few feet extra as needed. Cut paper.

9 Twist the paper to resemble a thick rope. Tape the paper to hold the rope shape, if necessary.

10 Use the uncovered wire ends to attach leaf boughs to the paper rope so leaves droop downward. Overlap leaf boughs to create a full, extravagant look.

11 Glue the oranges in place. Drape the garland on top of your mantel and secure with tape, if necessary.

TIPS:

* Save money by crushing up tissue paper or crepe paper instead of using Styrofoam balls.

* Store your garlands in plastic bins to enjoy them year after year.

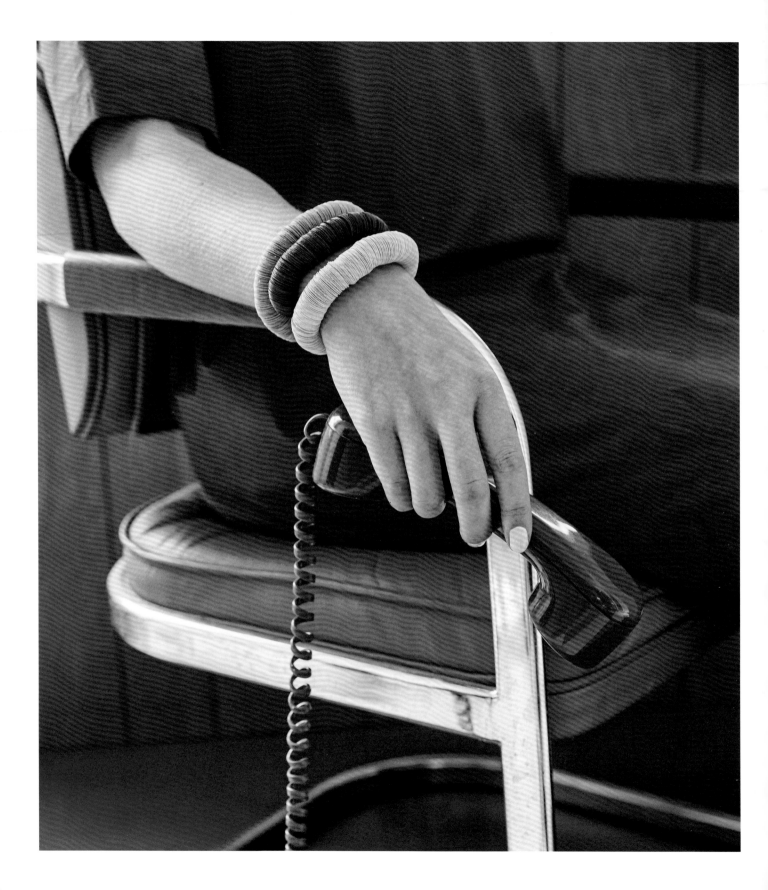

PAPER DISK BRACELET

I'm generally hesitant to craft paper fashion accessories for fear that they won't hold up to wear and tear. Well, like a protest march, there is strength in numbers! String a bunch of paper disks together and the end result is as strong as steel; you will worry much less about paper's supposed fragility. Plus, it's so easy: If you're a hesitant crafter, this project is for you. It's hard to go wrong. Wear a single bracelet, or pile on a few in different shades for more impact.

HOW TO USE ORANGE

If you don't want to use a classic orange but do want to stay in the orange family, add a touch of color from a nearby hue on the color wheel. Here, I used a range of colors: coral (orange with a pink tint) topped off with mint and forest green bracelets to ground it, and styled with a burnt orange. Desaturating—adding a complementary color, in this case blue, to dull the brightness—bright orange down to burnt orange makes the color more wearable and more harmonious with other colors.

COLORS

orange, coral, forest green, mint green

TIME

an episode of *The Office*

INSPIRATION

stone beads

(MATERIALS)

cardstock in various colors

¾-inch (2-cm) circle punch and mini hole punch, template, or paper-cutting machine

1-mm-wide elastic string

scissors

(INSTRUCTIONS)

1   Cut out 350 to 400 disks from cardstock, depending on the size of your wrist (about 350 if you're small-boned and 400 if you have a larger frame). You can do this with a circle punch, by hand using the template (see page 171), or with a paper-cutting machine. Make sure the hole in the center of the disks is large enough for your elastic to fit through. If you're cutting disks with a machine, make a ¾-inch (2-cm) disk, and slice a smaller disk onto the middle.

2   Thread the paper disks onto the elastic until it is long enough to fit around your wrist. The disks should be packed together very closely.

3   Cut the elastic, and secure the ends with a square knot. Trim ends. Wear in good health.

BALLOON ARCH WITH PAPER LEAVES

A few years ago, I created the first #LarsBalloonArch, an organically shaped arch that I draped over a dessert table. Floral designer Ashley Beyer added some gorgeous fresh flowers into the mix, and the project was a runaway success. To this day it is the number-one post on *The House That Lars Built*. The most satisfying part of creating this arch has been witnessing so many readers try out their own versions. I've seen them used at baby showers, weddings, and birthday parties. This project is perfect for any special occasion for which you want to put in a little extra effort. I wanted to try a version using paper florals rather than fresh blooms, and I love how it turned out. (Of course, it doesn't hurt to find an adorable pink house on which to showcase it.) Here, I created a standard doorframe arch and inserted handmade paper foliage to add a touch of glamour.

HOW TO USE ORANGE

Working with a color I'm not naturally drawn to, like orange, is a fun creative challenge. I like turning a color I'm not thrilled about into something stunning. My trick? Add colors I do love. In this case, I used the analogous hues pink and yellow.

COLORS

orange, coral, yellow, pink, gold

TIME

an evening of prep and a few hours of installation (Regina Spektor on repeat)

INSPIRATION

#LarsBalloonArch

(MATERIALS)

brown painter's paper

gaffer or heavy-duty duct tape, nails, or temporary sticky hooks

balloons in orange, coral, and pink, plus a few yellow, in various sizes

balloon pump

low-temperature glue gun (do not use a high-temperature one)

scissors

masking tape

5 feet (1.5 m) white butcher paper

gold spray paint

template (page 170)

white paper

pencil

craft knife

75 18-inch (46-cm) 22-gauge floral wires, cut into 4- to 5-inch (10- to 13-cm) pieces

50 18-inch (46-cm) 18-gauge floral wires

(INSTRUCTIONS)

A

ARCH

1 Twist the painter's paper like a rope, bend into a simple arch shape, and secure with tape.

2 Install the arch in your space using tape, nails, or temporary sticky hooks. I used gaffer tape, which is strong but does not leave a mark.

BALLOON CLUSTERS

1 Blow up the balloons to small, medium, and large sizes.

2 Glue together clusters of four to five different-size balloons. Leave the lip of one balloon free. Be sure to use a low-temperature glue gun.

3 Cut an 8-inch (20-cm) piece of masking tape and wrap 2 inches (5 cm) around the free lip of one balloon to create a tail.

4 Adhere balloon clusters to the arch with the tape tails. Fill in any gaps with additional balloons and tape.

B

LEAVES

1 Spray the butcher paper gold. Let it dry overnight.

2 Copy the template onto white paper, and cut out. Trace leaves onto gold paper, and cut out.

3 Use a craft knife to score the leaves down the middle.

C

ADDING THE LEAVES

1 Glue leaves onto 4- to 5-inch-long (10- to 13-cm) 22-gauge wires, leaving a 1- to 2-inch (2.5- to 5-cm) tail of wire at the bottom. Wrap 4 to 5 leaves around each 18-gauge wire. Insert leaf-covered wires among balloon clusters, twisting as needed to secure (D).

TIPS:

✳ *You can blow up the balloons before the installation. They will last even longer if you tie them extra tightly.*

✳ *Use only a low-temperature glue gun on balloons.*

✳ *One bunch of balloons covers about 2 square feet (0.6 square m). Determine whether your installation location needs nails, temporary sticky hooks, or strong tape. Use temporary sticky hooks on surfaces you don't want to harm.*

"**YELLOW** is the favorite color of crazy people.
At least that's what someone told me when I was a kid.
Which made me stop and think for a minute . . . But only a
minute before I quickly decided that I didn't care."

—EVA JORGENSEN, *Sycamore Street Press*

Ah! A sip of crisp lemonade, the bright sun of summer—it can only be effervescent YELLOW, *the color of happiness. Can you tell I'm slightly biased? I'd give it the first or second spot on my list of color favorites, depending on my mood and the time of year. As a teenager, I owned my fair share of* YELLOW *memorabilia thanks to the pervasive sunflower trend. This included my favorite sunflower-print hat and matching vest and shorts. It also may have made an appearance as a part of a team uniform for a clogging festival I somehow signed up for, but we're not here to talk about past mistakes.*

FUN FACTS ABOUT YELLOW:

→ YELLOW IS KNOWN TO MAKE BABIES CRY MORE BECAUSE IT IS SAID TO ACTIVATE THE BRAIN. WORD TO THE WISE: PAINT THE NURSERY A COLOR OTHER THAN YELLOW! → IN INDIA, YELLOW IS A SYMBOL OF PEACE AND KNOWLEDGE. → ONE OF J.M.W. TURNER'S FAVORITE COLORS TO USE WAS INDIAN YELLOW, A PIGMENT THAT HAILED FROM THE INDIAN STATE BIHAR. THE COLOR WAS DERIVED FROM THE URINE OF COWS OR BUFFALO THAT HAD EATEN THE LEAVES OF MANGO TREES. THE URINE WAS THEN ADDED TO CLAY AND FORMED INTO ROUNDISH SHAPES. THESE BALLS WERE GROUND DOWN AND BLENDED WITH ACACIA GUM TO PRODUCE TURNER'S BELOVED PAINT. THE MORE YOU KNOW . . .

FLORAL HIMMELI CHANDELIER

While on a work trip to Helsinki, I visited a small old-fashioned teahouse outside the city for some afternoon tea. The old yellow house was situated in a luscious green meadow and featured rustic folk detailing along the rooflines. There was a porch with rockers where diners took in the late summer afternoon, the loveliest time of the year in the northern countries. It felt like a cozy visit to Grandma's house. Afterward, we were treated to traditional folk dancing by a local chapter of the Finnish Folk Society, who were dressed in their vibrant costumes. Somehow I was convinced to join (while wearing my rainbow-striped jumpsuit).

Inside I spotted some geometric shapes made from straws. I later learned they are a traditional craft called *himmeli*, which is typically used as décor during Christmastime. I've been enamored with himmeli ever since that afternoon in the teahouse. This yellow himmeli is a simplified version made from paper straws, paper beads, and paper flowers. Feel free to try out your own shapes and colors.

HOW TO USE YELLOW

I'll never forget the moment I fell in love with mustard yellow. I had returned home from living abroad long enough to be out of touch with current American styles. My sister greeted me at the airport wearing a mustard yellow sweater. I had never contemplated this color, and I kept gazing at her, trying to make sense of it, when I got it. Mustard is the neutral of yellows! It can be used in the autumnal palette of deep reds and pinks or alongside a gorgeous navy blue. Here, it's paired with a beautiful gray-blue to freshen it up.

COLORS

yellow and blue

TIME

Songs You'd Sing in the Shower playlist

INSPIRATION

Scandinavian Christmas decorations

(MATERIALS)

templates (page 171)

white paper

scissors

pencil

yellow lined legal pad

22 felt balls in yellow and gray-blue

glue gun

1 8-inch (20-cm) embroidery hoop

1 10-inch (25-cm) embroidery hoop

cornflower blue yarn

yellow cardstock

150 ¼-inch (6-mm) wooden beads

4 shades of yellow acrylic paint

1-inch (2.5-cm) foam paintbrush

1 1-inch (2.5-cm) wooden bead

gray-blue acrylic paint

40 paper straws, cut into 2-inch (5-cm) lengths

twine

12 clothespins

4 by 4-inch (10 by 10-cm) piece of cardboard

tapestry needle

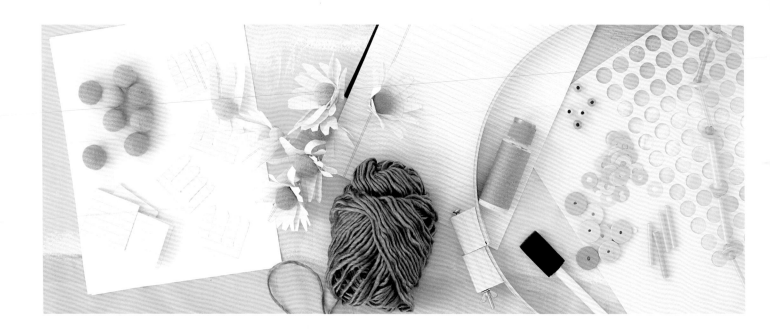

{ INSTRUCTIONS }

1 Copy the petal template onto white paper, and cut out. Trace the petal onto yellow legal paper, and cut out five petals per flower (A).

2 Gently wrap each of the five daisy petals around a felt ball, pleating the paper as you go and securing with glue (B). Make 22 daisies total, and set aside.

3 Wrap the embroidery hoops tightly with yarn, covering completely. Secure the ends with glue. Glue 12 daisies to the larger hoop and 10 to the smaller hoop, spacing evenly (see photo on previous page).

4 Copy the circle template onto white paper, and cut out. Trace onto yellow cardstock, and cut out 500 paper disks, or use a circle punch and hole punch. Paint the small wooden beads in various

shades of yellow and the large (1-inch / 2.5-cm) wooden bead blue. Let dry. Paint the straw pieces in various shades of yellow. Let dry.

5 Cut six lengths of twine to about 4 feet (1.2 m) long each. Thread the cut straws, paper disks, and yellow beads onto each piece of twine in a pattern of your choice. Leave a 4-inch (10-cm) tail uncovered on each piece (C). Use a clothespin to temporarily secure each end and prevent the straws and beads from falling off.

6 About 12 inches (30.5 cm) from the bottom, glue each piece of twine to the inside of the larger embroidery hoop, spacing evenly. Glue the twine to the smaller embroidery hoop, leaving about 12 inches (30.5 cm) between the hoops.

ASSEMBLING THE CHANDELIER

7 Gather the excess twine at the top. Cut a long length of yarn (determined by how high or low you would like to hang your himmeli). Tie the length of yarn around the gathered twine and secure tightly with several knots. Trim excess ends from the beaded twine, but leave the yarn ends to hang your himmeli. Gather the excess twine at the bottom and secure by tying a knot.

ADDING THE YARN TASSEL

8 Create a yarn tassel by wrapping the yarn about 20 times around the piece of cardboard. Carefully slip the yarn loops off of the piece of cardboard. Use your fingers to pinch the bundle of yarn loops about 1 inch (2.5 cm)

down from one end of the loops. Cut a 7-inch (18-cm) length of yarn and wrap it tightly around the bundle of loops 5 to 10 times at the spot where you have pinched the loops together. Tie 3 tight knots and bring the ends of the string down to blend in with the loops. Cut the other ends of the yarn loops to form the tassel ends. Trim the tassel ends to a uniform length. Thread the tapestry needle with a 7-inch (18-cm) length of twine. Thread the twine through the looped end of the tassel until the tassel is centered along the length of twine. Tie 2 tight knots. Thread the tail ends of the twine through the blue bead and use the twine to tie the tassel to the ends of the beaded strings. Trim all excess twine (D).

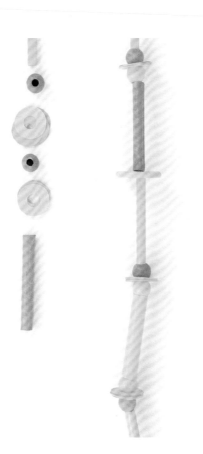

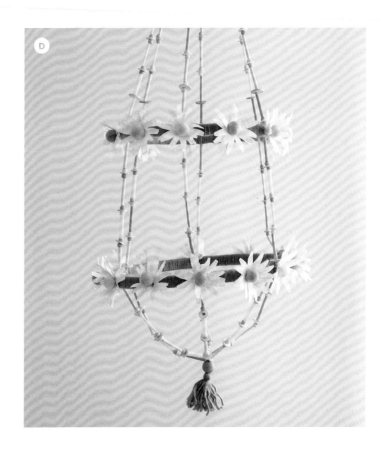

CUPCAKE LINER SHOE CLIPS

There are certain childhood habits I just can't drop, like dressing up for holidays and parties (remember school spirit days?). This cupcake liner shoe clip is one such example. It's especially cheery for a party.

HOW TO USE YELLOW

The cupcake liner is a juvenile bright yellow, so I chose a desaturated color palette to accompany it. Every shade of the warm spectrum is represented—pink, red, orange, yellow—set against a cool palette of periwinkle pointed heels.

COLORS

bright yellow, coral pink, burnt orange, burgundy, periwinkle

TIME

an episode or two of Radiolab

INSPIRATION

antique shoe clips

(MATERIALS)

- 4 1¼-inch (3-cm) diameter cupcake liners
- scissors
- glue gun
- 2 wooden disks 1½ inches (4 cm) in diameter
- acrylic or house paint in coral pink and deep burgundy
- paintbrush
- ¾-inch (2-cm) drill bit
- 2 wooden disks 1 inch (2.5 cm) in diameter
- painter's tape
- 2 shoe clips

(INSTRUCTIONS)

1 Fold a cupcake liner in half.

2 Cut about 1 inch (2.5 cm) into the liner at the groove lines. Repeat on a second cup.

3 Layer one cup on top of the other and glue together. Let dry. Repeat steps 1 through 3.

4 Paint the two larger wooden disks coral pink. Let dry.

5 If needed, drill into the center of the smaller disks to create holes. Cover half of a smaller wooden disk with painter's tape. Paint the other half burgundy. Repeat on the other smaller disk. Let dry, and remove tape.

6 Glue the smaller disks on top of the larger. Let dry. Glue the cupcake liners to cover half the bottoms of the backs of the larger disks. Let dry.

7 Glue the shoe clips to bottoms of the backs of the larger disks. Let dry before attaching to shoes.

PAPER NEON SIGN

This sign may lack the illuminating capabilities of neon, but it makes up for that in charm. Displaying a mantra or a baby name immediately personalizes a space. Use fluorescent crepe paper, or spray-paint it for more brightness.

HOW TO USE YELLOW

Yellow can be included in many combinations, but is beautiful on its own. A bright yellow can fill a whole space.

COLORS

bright yellow

TIME

watching the film *True Stories*

INSPIRATION

classic neon sign

(MATERIALS)

18-gauge wire spool

wire cutters

medium backer rod (a light, easily moldable foam tubing used to fill gaps or cracks under doors or in windows, available at hardware stores)

craft knife

masking tape

160-gram florist crepe paper

scissors

glue gun

(INSTRUCTIONS)

Write your word on a sheet of paper in the style you want it. Print a template to your preferred size. The one shown is 2½ feet (76 cm). I printed the template at a copy center as a black-and-white engineer print.

Fold over the wire so it is double thick. You can do this in small segments.

1 Using the template as your guide, bend the wire so it spells out the word you have chosen. Cut the excess wire.

2 Slice the backer rod in half lengthwise with your craft knife (A).

3 Slide the backer rod onto the wire. Don't hot glue the backer rod to the wire or it will melt (B). Instead, use masking tape to secure the backer rod around the wire every 2 inches (5 cm) or so. Do this as you work, and it won't unravel as you're going around corners.

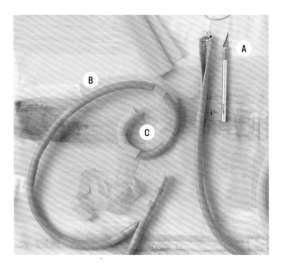

4 Check the letters against the template, and adjust the wire.

5 Cut the crepe paper about ¾ inch (2 cm) against the grain and gently stretch it (C).

6 Glue the edge of the crepe paper to the start of the letter, and wrap around the letter. Do this letter by letter with multiple strips, overlapping the strips so they appear continuous. Be gentle enough that the paper doesn't rip and firm enough that it doesn't bubble.

"When I am surrounded by greenery I feel at once calm, fresh, and reinvigorated."

—JUSTINA BLAKENEY *of TheJungalow.com*

In elementary school, I read in a magazine that forest **GREEN** *was the color of the school year. I didn't know that there are companies whose purpose is to set color trends, so I found it interesting that someone could know in advance what color would be stocked in stores. "Do they have magical powers?" I wondered. Sure enough, forest* **GREEN** *was everywhere, and of course I followed the trend, secure in the knowledge that I was cool because I had read about it months earlier. Despite falling victim to consumer marketing, I grew to love forest* **GREEN***. I haven't worn it since I was a kid, but I'm waiting for its return in the trend cycle.*

FUN FACTS ABOUT GREEN:

→ **GREEN** HAS LONG BEEN A SYMBOL OF FERTILITY AND WAS ONCE THE PREFERRED COLOR CHOICE FOR WEDDING GOWNS IN THE 1400S (THINK JAN VAN EYCK'S *ARNOLFINI PORTRAIT*). → BEFORE THE 1950S SANTA'S SUIT WAS **GREEN**—UNTIL COCA-COLA CHANGED HIS OUTFIT TO RED. → IN ONE ROOM AT THE WHITE HOUSE, THOMAS JEFFERSON ADDED A **GREEN** FLOOR CLOTH TO THE SPACE. JOHN QUINCY ADAMS THEN INSTALLED GREEN DRAPERIES AND UPHOLSTERED PIECES, AND SOON IT BECAME KNOWN AS THE GREEN ROOM.

ORIGAMI MONEY LEI

Do you find yourself wondering what to give as a graduation gift? Money, of course, is the go-to, but I always want to do something more personal. More recently, I've noticed the advent of leis made from origami cash, the perfect blend of a practical and thoughtful handmade gift. You can also use play money.

HOW TO USE GREEN

I am fascinated with bright and clever foreign currency. (Have you seen the Canadian bills? They're see-through!) I find it odd that U.S. currency is monochromatic. Apparently, this is because the green is resistant to destruction and fading and difficult to counterfeit. Artistically, because the green is so muted and set against off-white, it becomes a neutral when paired with more vibrant colors.

Here I used the palette of the tropics, including flamingo and pale pink. I added in two shades of green leaves to boost the feeling—forest green and blue-green.

COLORS

money green, blue-green,
deep green, pink

TIME

watching *Funny Face*

INSPIRATION

Hawaiian lei

(MATERIALS)

white paper

pencil

wooden beads (twenty 8 mm, sixteen 10 mm, four 20 mm, two 25 mm)

pink acrylic or house paint in two shades of pink

rough paintbrush or foam brush

12 bills in the amount of your choosing (I recommend getting fresh bills from the bank, which fold more crisply)

templates (page 171)

scissors

pink cardstock

22-gauge floral wire spool

wire cutters

pink floral stamen (three per flower); see Resources, page 189

glue gun

blue-green cardstock

⅛- or 1/16-inch (3- or 1.5-mm) hole punch

green embroidery floss

gold thread

PAINTING THE BEADS

1 Paint all beads one of two shades of pink, and set aside to dry.

ORIGAMI LEAVES

1 Start with George Washington (or whatever face is on your bill) right side up and facing you.

2 Fold in the bottom corners until they meet the top edge of the bill. This will form a diagonal line that extends from the top corner on each side (A, B).

3 Universally fold (see page 19) the bill in half horizontally to create a horizontal crease through George's nose. Unfold, and then universally fold in half each of the halves so you have four parallel horizontal segments. Repeat so you have eight segments (C).

4 Accordion fold all the folds with valley folds (see page 19) on the top and bottom (D). Fold in half vertically so both sides of the long top edge are touching (E).

5 Tuck the top lip of one of the top edges over the other. While holding the top together, compress some of the pleats at the base to create a leaf shape (F). If you want extra stability, fold over the tip of the leaf so the tucked layer is locked in place.

TIP: *If you start with crisp bills, the folding process will be much easier and your end product will look better.*

FLOWERS

1 Copy the template onto white paper, and cut out. Trace onto pink cardstock, and cut out five flowers. Curl the edges of each petal around a pencil or a paintbrush handle.

2 Cut five 3-inch (7.5-cm) pieces of floral wire.

3 Form a ¼-inch (6-mm) loop with the wire and twist the ends together (G).

4 Lay the wire on the flower so the loop is on the outside and the twisted ends come through the hole.

5 Glue a stamen to the twisted ends.

6 Wrap the flower around the stamen and glue the flap on one petal to the inside of the adjacent petal. Repeat for remaining flowers (H).

CARDSTOCK LEAVES

1 Copy the template onto white paper, and cut out. Trace onto blue-green and forest green cardstock, and cut out 40 leaves.

2 Use the hole punch to make a hole at the base of the leaves.

ASSEMBLING THE LEI

1 Cut 4 pieces of embroidery floss to lengths of 9 inches (23 cm), 10 inches (25 cm), 13 inches (33 cm), and 14 inches (35.5 cm). Tie a knot at one end of each piece of floss, leaving a 1- to 1½-inch (2.5 to 4 cm) tail.

2 For the 9-inch (23 cm) and the 14-inch (35.5 cm) pieces of embroidery floss, thread on a paper leaf and slide it down so it sits next to the knot you just made.

3 Slide the floss through the center hole of a money leaf, and tie a knot to secure it in place, ¼ inch to ½ inch (6 mm to 1.3 cm) from the paper leaf.

4 Alternate between paper leaves and money leaves, securing the money leaves with knots. Space the leaves evenly throughout the entire length of floss. End with a knot, leaving a 1- to 1½-inch (2.5 to 4 cm) tail.

5 For the 10-inch (25.5 cm) piece of embroidery floss, thread a paper leaf and slide it to the knot at the end. Tie a knot on the other side of the leaf, about ¼ inch (6 mm) from the initial knot, to keep the leaf from sliding around too much. Repeat this step until you have three leaves separated by knots.

6 Slide on a paper flower and tie a knot. Continue a pattern of three leaves, one flower until you have used all five flowers. End with a knot, leaving a 1- to 1½-inch (2.5 to 4 cm) tail.

7 For the 13-inch (33-cm) piece of embroidery floss, thread only green paper leaves, separating them with evenly spaced ¼- to ½-inch (6-mm to 1.3-cm) knots. End with a knot, leaving 1- to 1½-inch (2.5- to 4-cm) tail.

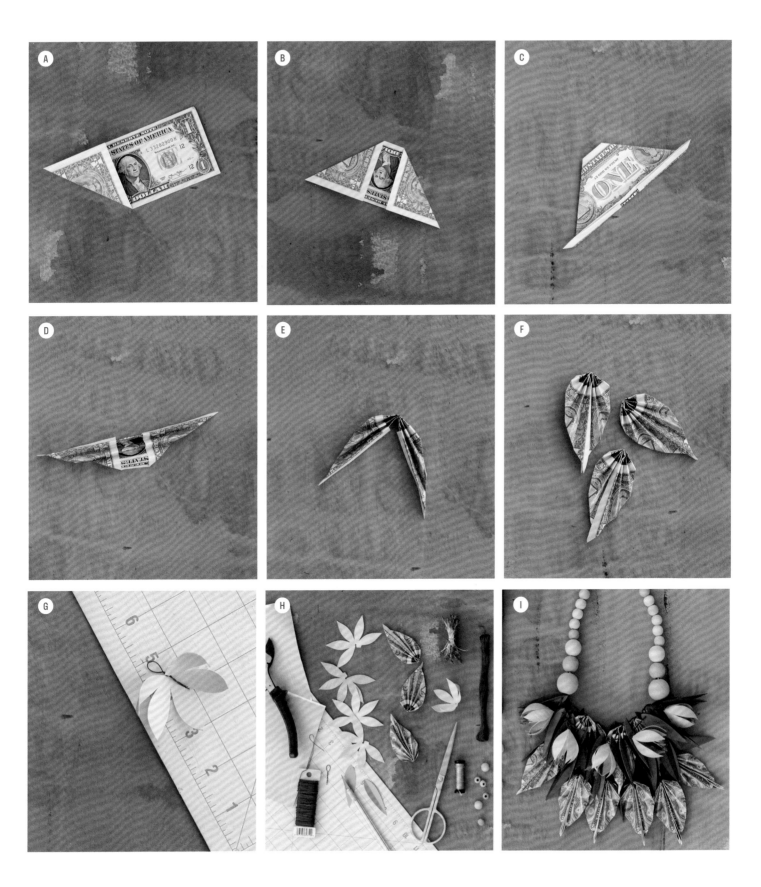

PARTY GOODS MANDALA

Nepal is one of the most intriguing and art-infused places I have ever visited. I had the great opportunity to learn about the culture and design aesthetic from some local experts and was intrigued by the storytelling of the Buddhist and Hindu art. A common theme was the *mandala*, a geometric pattern or chart representing the universe. The mandala was a popular motif even before the coloring book trend took hold a few years ago, and it has been applied in many artful ways. Here, I used party supplies to create a beautiful backdrop décor.

HOW TO USE GREEN

One of my favorite color combinations is kelly green against mint green. Ever since pastels came back onto the scene a few years ago, I love pairing a pastel with a deeper color in the same family: blush with hot pink, pale yellow with bright yellow, baby blue with navy. It works every time!

COLORS

kelly green and mint green

TIME

a few of my favorite party playlists

INSPIRATION

mandala

(INSTRUCTIONS)

Start at the middle of the mandala and work your way outward, attaching the objects per the template with sticky tack. Optional: Use a projector to project the template onto the wall so you can ensure exact placement.

TIP: *To save your mandala for another party, package it in plastic bags, labeled by section.*

(MATERIALS)

template (page 187)

pack of sticky tack

50 paper green-and-white straws

32 green toothpicks

32 green twist ties

16 3-inch (7.5-cm) paper circles

16 1½-inch (4-cm) paper circles

32 1½-inch paper teardrops

12 packages palm tree food picks (136 total)

16 green cups

4 7-inch green paper plates

8 green party horns

17 4-inch (10-cm) tissue paper fans

4 12-inch (30.5-cm) honeycomb diamonds

16 green plastic forks

16 2-inch (5-cm) honeycomb tissue balls

16 green number candles

CURTAIN TASSEL TIEBACK

Extravagant French tassel tiebacks have always fascinated me. So much ornament is packed in something that serves a seemingly limited purpose. This crepe paper tassel is my (much cheaper) version of the opulent French original. Have fun selecting various wood shapes and ribbons to mix in with it.

HOW TO USE GREEN

The teal crepe paper I used here fits in nicely with other jewel tones, like reds, blues, yellows, and purples. If you pick a strong hue, tone it down by desaturating. I warmed up the cool tone of the green with tomato red and orchid purple, which has a lot of red in it. Gold leaf adds a dash of shine. It's all set off by a beautiful chartreuse green.

COLORS

blue-green, chartreuse, tomato red,
metallic gold, orchid purple

TIME

an episode of *Chef's Table*

INSPIRATION

antique French curtain tiebacks

(MATERIALS)

180-gram teal crepe paper

scissors

glue gun

87 to 90 inches (220 to 230 cm) thin rope or cord

3 skeins green embroidery floss

8 inches (20 cm) green velvet ribbon

large wooden beads: 2 large spheres, 2 small spheres, 2 squares, 4 disks

acrylic paint in purple, red, and teal

paintbrush

gold leaf kit

10 to 12 skeins teal embroidery floss

(INSTRUCTIONS)

1. Cut crepe paper into two 5-inch-tall (13-cm) and 39- to 59-inch-wide (100- to 150-cm) strips. Choose your width based on how thick you want your tassel to be. Create ½-inch-wide (1.3-cm) fringe by cutting 4 inches (10 cm) into the crepe paper strips. The cuts should be parallel to the grain of the paper.

2. Glue one end of the rope to the unfringed edge of one piece of crepe paper.

3. Begin rolling the crepe paper tightly, beginning at the edge with the glued rope. The rope will end up in the middle of the tassel (3A+3B).

4. Use green embroidery floss to wrap the top of the tassel 20 to 25 times. Secure with glue (4A+4B).

5. Wrap ribbon on top of the green embroidery floss. Secure with glue.

6. Paint wooden beads in various colors and gold leaf. Let dry. Thread half the beads onto the rope so they sit right above the tassel. Thread the other half of the beads onto the other end of the rope. Leave about 1 inch (2.5 cm) of rope below the last bead.

7. Repeat steps 2 through 5 to create the other tassel.

8. Wrap the length of the rope with the teal embroidery floss, covering it completely. Secure with glue at both ends.

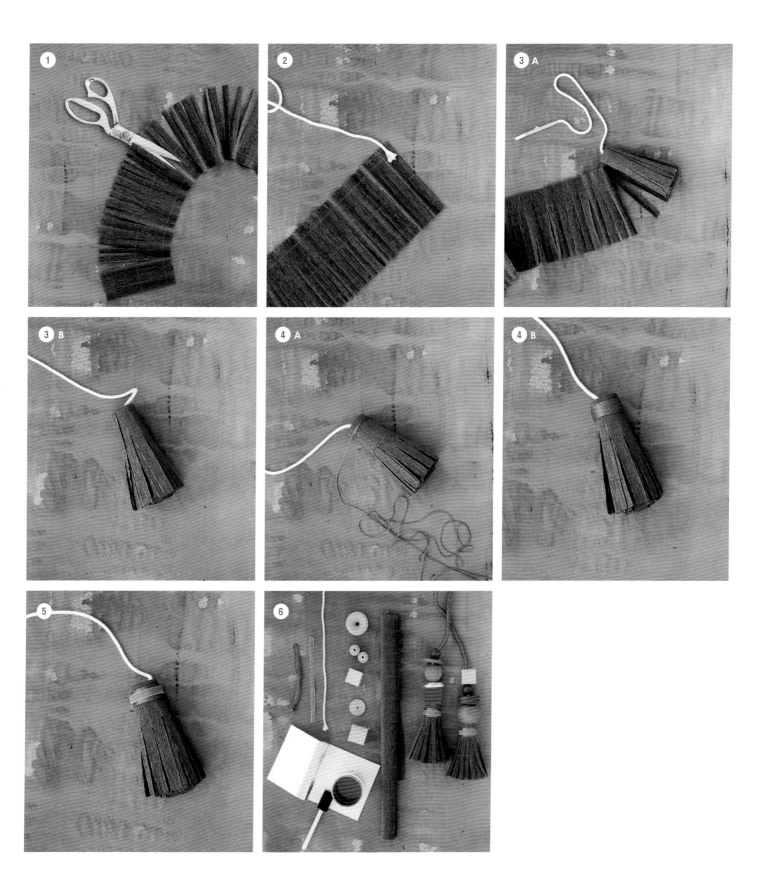

"Every day I have a different color jostling for favorite.
Today, as I look out at the waves at Wategos Beach,
it is turquoise. Nature offers the best colors!"

—SIBELLA COURT, *stylist*

I grew up in Dana Point, a small harbor town in Southern California known for its water sports and beach culture. Birthdays, daily hangouts, and family pictures all took place on the beach; schedules centered around the tides; our high school mascot was the dolphin; and our colors were **BLUE** *and silver. Yet, I've always had a bit of wanderlust and a strong pull from other directions. I've lived all around the world since then, but you can't take the beach town out of the girl. That point where the milky* **BLUE** *sky meets the steel* **BLUE** *ocean is still home.*

FUN FACTS ABOUT BLUE:

→ **BLUE** IS A COLOR OF OPPOSITES—IT REPRESENTS THE WORKING CLASS AS WELL AS ROYALTY. → ALFRED HITCHCOCK ONCE HOSTED AN ALL-**BLUE** DINNER PARTY. EVERYTHING FROM THE FLOWERS TO THE TABLECLOTH TO THE UTENSILS TO THE FOOD WAS **BLUE**, INCLUDING THE STEAKS. → THE RUSSIAN LANGUAGE USES TWO WORDS FOR **BLUE**. ONE MEANS DARK **BLUE** AND THE OTHER MEANS LIGHT **BLUE**.

DIP-DYED PAPER FLOWERS

Viewing commonplace objects in a new light comes in handy when you are planning a wedding but also working within a budget. Instead of ordering a fresh floral altarpiece, which is undeniably beautiful but also expensive, make your own out of coffee filters and soufflé and medicine cups. You'll save on floral costs, and you'll also have a ball creating it with your friends and family.

HOW TO USE BLUE

Various shades of blues always work well together—think of the sky meeting the ocean. Don't be afraid to add in some green for depth.

COLORS

monochromatic blues with a touch of blue-green

TIME

a night to dye, a day to dry, and an afternoon to install

INSPIRATION

Impressionist landscape

(MATERIALS)

¼ to ½ cup (60 to 120 ml) house paint or acrylic paint in shades of blue and teal (I used three colors)

1 quart-size (1 L) bucket for each paint color you choose

water

packs of paper soufflé cups, medicine cups, and coffee filters in various sizes; about 30 per strand, 40 strands total

drop cloth

template (page 172)

white paper

scissors

pencil

silver paper (or white paper spray-painted silver)

sewing machine

craft needle

embroidery floss or twine

glue gun

(INSTRUCTIONS)

DYEING

1 Dilute your paint in buckets of water using a 1-to-1 ratio to create a dye.

2 Submerge the soufflé and medicine cups in the dye. Remove some after a few minutes, and let others soak so you get a variety of shades. Dip the filters only about halfway; the dye will bleed to create an ombré effect.

3 Let all the cups and filters dry on a drop cloth for 24 hours.

A SILVER LEAF GARLANDS

1 Copy the template onto white paper, and cut out. Trace onto silver paper, and cut out about 100 leaves.

2 Run the leaves continuously through a sewing machine, leaving some thread space between each leaf.

B FILTER GARLANDS

1 Cut a 6- to 8-foot (2- to 2.5-m) length of embroidery floss.

2 Fold the filters in half and then in half again.

3 Unfold a filter once. Place the floss in the crease and secure with a drop of glue at the top of the filter.

4 Fold the filter around the thread.

5 Continue, spacing the filters 1 to 3 inches (2.5 to 7.5 cm) apart, until the embroidery floss is covered.

C CUP GARLANDS

1 Thread a craft needle with a 6- to 8-foot (2- to 2.5-m) length of embroidery floss.

2 Use the needle to puncture a hole in the middle of the base of a cup, then slide the cup to the end of the floss. Secure with a dot of glue.

3 Continue, spacing the cups 1 to 3 inches (2.5 to 7.5 cm) apart, until the embroidery floss is covered.

INSTALLATION

Drape the garlands over an altar or a rod. Cluster like garlands together and vary the lengths.

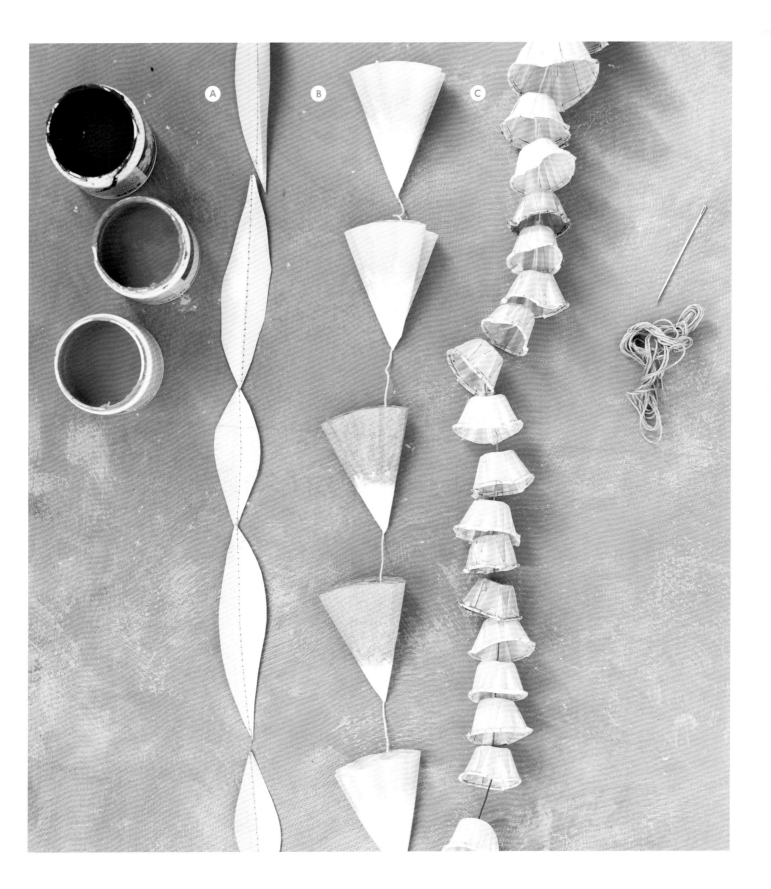

FLORAL SUNPRINT

I was honored to visit the home of a pressed-flower collector. The house included several floor-to-ceiling cupboards with flat drawers. Each drawer contained a box with various types of pressed flowers that the owner and his family had collected over the decades. He let me buy a box, which I still treasure, and I've been experimenting with all sorts of flowers ever since.

One way I've used them is with sun printing, which employs the sun to set the deep blue color. I created designs based on Scandinavian symmetrical folk patterns. With sun printing you must lay down your patterns quickly because once the cyanotype paper is exposed to the sun, the pattern starts to set. Spend some time working out your design on a piece of acrylic first, and attach glue dots to hold it in place. When you're ready, set the acrylic on your paper and let the sun do the rest.

HOW TO USE BLUE

Sun printing involves placing objects on white cyanotype paper and letting the sun make a print; anything not blocked out will turn blue. I chose cyanotype paper that turns a deeper blue, which feels moodier than the brighter ultramarine. This classic combination cannot be beat.

COLORS

cerulean blue

TIME

Hollywood Reporter roundtable videos on YouTube

INSPIRATION

pressed wildflowers

(MATERIALS)

pressed flowers

18 by 24-inch (46 by 61-cm) piece of acrylic (you can get this from the hardware store)

glue dots

26 by 30-inch (66 by 76-cm) sheet of cyanotype paper

(INSTRUCTIONS)

1 Create your pattern by arranging pressed flowers on one side of the acrylic. Make sure the design fits. Secure the flowers with glue dots.

2 Lay the cyanotype paper flat on the ground in a spot that gets direct sunlight.

3 Position the acrylic on the cyanotype paper and set it in place.

4 Leave in the sun for about 20 minutes, or until the design has set.

5 Rinse the cyanotype paper with water, and let it fully dry.

PAPER BROOCH AND EARRINGS

Fashion is a huge source of inspiration for my work. Recently I've been inspired by the creative director of Gucci, Alessandro Michele, who pairs unexpected patterns and motifs in a glamorous yet historical way. There's always an elevated handmade element to his work that shows his experience working with needlepoint or crochet. In an interview in the June 2015 issue of *Vogue*, he described his vision for the brand as being influenced by his mother, who worked in the film industry. He described her as a "supercrazy lady, from this superstylish movie world. There is something eccentric about people like her that we miss today, so I built my fashion around the idea of individuality. The way you dress is really the way you feel, the way you live, what you read, your choices."

I wanted to translate this idea into something more accessible and friendly for your pocketbook, so I designed paper brooches and earrings that you can customize to your wardrobe. They're so easy to make that you can create one for every occasion. Get inspired by your favorite fashion to customize it to your own tastes.

HOW TO USE BLUE

Blues work well with the rest of the cool palette, so I chose various shades of blue and blue-green, as well as metallic silver.

COLORS

blues and metallic silver

TIME

one TED Talk

INSPIRATION

antique brooches

(MATERIALS)

templates (pages 172–73)

cardstock in three shades of blue and silver

scissors

glue stick

glue gun

pin or earrings backings

gloss finishes (optional)

(INSTRUCTIONS)

1　Copy the templates onto cardstock, and cut around each piece.

2　Use a glue stick to adhere the pieces to one another, as shown at right.

3　Use a glue gun to attach the pin or earring backing to the paper design.

4　If you'd like to protect the paper, apply thin, even coats of adhesive to finish it off.

*"O beautiful for spacious skies, / For amber waves of grain, /
For* **PURPLE** *mountain majesties"*

—"AMERICA THE BEAUTIFUL," *Samuel A. Ward*

When it comes to **PURPLE**, *I'm often at a loss as to how to incorporate it into my life. It is a color full of power and presence and requires a careful eye to incorporate it into a design. The deep pigment of grape juice refuses to go unnoticed, as does the overwhelming smell of lavender.* **PURPLE** *is strong! Over the years, I have taken note of* **PURPLE** *color combinations that I like, so I was reluctantly confident that it could be done. What did I find? Well, just like there is no bad weather, only inappropriate clothing, there are no ugly colors, only inappropriate combinations. I'm happy to report that I have found wonderful ways to use* **PURPLE**. *In this chapter I show you some of my findings.*

FUN FACTS ABOUT PURPLE:

→ **PURPLE** WAS THE COLOR OF THE FIRST HUMAN-MADE DYE. IT WAS CREATED FROM COAL TAR AND CALLED *MAUVEINE*. WILLIAM HENRY PERKIN DISCOVERED THE FORMULA IN 1856. → LEONARDO DA VINCI BELIEVED THAT THE POWER OF MEDITATION INCREASES TEN TIMES WHEN DONE IN A **PURPLE** LIGHT, AS IN THE **PURPLE** LIGHT OF STAINED GLASS. → GREEK POET HOMER DESCRIBED SEEING SINGLE-HUE RAINBOWS, WITH ONLY THE COLOR **PURPLE**.

FLORAL CUTOUT MOBILES

Matisse was the father of large-scale paper cutting. During the last ten years of his life he explored this new medium by painting sheets of white paper with gouache and cutting them into various shapes before pinning them to their permanent homes. He considered his cutouts the fulfillment of a lifelong ambition to create monumental works.

Here's my take on Matisse's magnificent paper cutouts: floral cutout mobiles. They would be lovely decorations in a child's room, by a window, or for a party.

HOW TO USE PURPLE

Red is probably my favorite companion for purple. I used a warm purple to go with a more orange-y red. It works every time! You can experiment with different shades of purples and it will still look top-notch.

COLORS

purples and reds

TIME

watching *La La Land*
for the fourth time

INSPIRATION

folk elements

(MATERIALS)

- poster board
- acrylic paint in reds and purples
- paintbrush
- templates (pages 174–75)
- white paper
- scissors
- pencil
- craft knife
- cutting mat
- 1⁄16-inch (1.5-mm) hole punch
- metal jump rings (jump rings are easy to remove, so do not use this in the rooms of young children who might swallow them)

(INSTRUCTIONS)

1. Texturize poster board by painting on designs like stripes, dots, and splatters.

2. Copy the templates onto white paper, and cut out. Trace onto poster board, and cut out the shapes with a craft knife.

3. Punch holes at the base and top of the flowers.

4. Insert the metal rings and connect three to five flowers. Hang from the ceiling or a wall.

PRINTABLE BOTANICAL WALLPAPER

The best part of high school biology was the beautiful old plant illustrations hung along the classroom walls. This is where I first fell in love with the poppy. I have since amassed my own collection of vintage botanical posters, but I also discovered a goldmine of online botanical libraries that have digitized their collections. Most of these books were published between the seventeenth and nineteenth centuries, so they are in the public domain. I printed off dozens of my favorites as a fun alternative to wallpaper.

HOW TO USE PURPLE

Much like orange, my trick for working with a less-favored color is to think about how it's used in nature. My favorite way to incorporate purple is, not surprisingly, through flowers. I adore purple flowers—all shades of them. Dusty purple combined with various shades of green is soul melting. I included some deep reds for variety.

COLORS

purple, green, red

TIME

listening to Beck's *Morning Phase*

INSPIRATION

botanical library

(MATERIALS)

downloadable files (found on *The House That Lars Built*; search "purple botanical wallpaper," or look for your own on botanical library databases or in vintage books)

scissors

sticky tack or glue

(INSTRUCTIONS)

1 Print files of the artwork. There are more than 100 from which to choose on *The House That Lars Built*.

2 Cut white surrounding borders off artwork.

3 Affix to the wall, starting at the bottom and working upward.

Optional: To add some dimension, curl the edges of the pages with a smooth pencil or a paintbrush handle.

PAINT CHIP TILE BACKDROP

When I lived in Denmark, one of my favorite things to do was observe the way people dressed. Over time I started to notice that some older women were wearing head-to-toe purple: purple pants, purple coat, purple scarves, purple glasses. I love a woman who wears her passion with confidence! This all-purple paint-chip backdrop is easy (and cheap!) to produce because of the endless hues of paint chips available at home-improvement stores. Create a purple theme for your next party, and use all-purple accents to drive it home.

HOW TO USE PURPLE

As per the purple-clad ladies, a surefire way to use any color successfully is to employ it monochromatically—that is, with other shades of the same color. Your project will always feel cohesive and well thought-out when you stick with one hue. You're exploring the depths, so it's still visually interesting.

COLORS

monochromatic purples

TIME

an evening binge-watching
Parks and Recreation

INSPIRATION

glass mosaic

(MATERIALS)

various shades of purple paint chips

1-inch (2.5-cm) square paper punch

glue or sticky tack

(INSTRUCTIONS)

Punch squares from the paint chips. Glue them to a backdrop or sticky tack them to a wall.

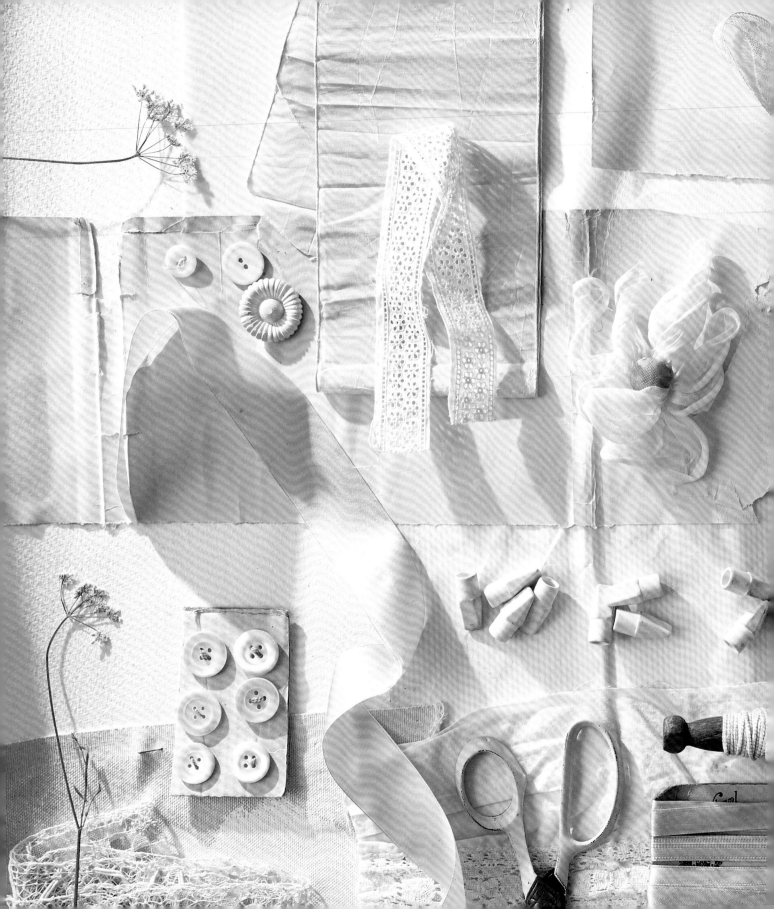

"WHITE is like the middle child to its eclectic rainbow siblings: optimistic, nurturing, and a peacekeeper."

—KENDRA SMOOT, *stylist*

WHITE is not an official color of the rainbow—the lucky seven are red, orange, yellow, green, blue, indigo, and violet. In fact, WHITE is not a color at all, but rather the wavelengths of all the colors combined. In a book about color and rainbows, you would think being a color would be one of the most important criteria for inclusion, but WHITE has an intriguing story to tell. After all, we couldn't see all those beautiful colors if it wasn't for WHITE light. WHITE literally lights the way, and it goes even further than that. Typically, white assists in the storytelling of other colors. For example, it is commonly used as a basic backdrop in photography, as a lightener for mixing paints, or as a clothing uniform (WHITE shirt, jeans, done!). WHITE makes the rest of the colors look good.

FUN FACTS ABOUT WHITE:

→ THE WHITE HOUSE IS TOUCHED UP EVERY YEAR WITH 570 GALLONS OF BRIGHT WHITE PAINT. → IN THE EARLY MODERN ERA, WIDOWS WORE WHITE TO INDICATE THEY WERE IN MOURNING. THE WIDOWS OF THE KINGS OF FRANCE WORE WHITE UNTIL ANNE OF BRITTANY HALTED THE TRADITION IN THE SIXTEENTH CENTURY. MANY KNIGHTS WORE A WHITE TUNIC, ALONG WITH A RED CLOAK, WHICH INDICATED THEY WERE WILLING TO GIVE THEIR BLOOD FOR THE KING OR THE CHURCH. → WHITE IS NOT TECHNICALLY A COLOR, BUT CONTAINS ALL THE WAVELENGTHS OF VISIBLE LIGHT. BLACK, ON THE OTHER HAND, IS THE ABSENCE OF VISIBLE LIGHT.

WHITE PAPER SCULPTURE

While visiting Toronto, I popped into a Japanese paper store that carried everything an aspiring bookbinder and paper lover could ever desire. Artfully arranged on the walls and ceilings were countless paper-folding techniques and origami shapes. The intricacy of the expert folds created a quiet reverence in the shop. It's amazing that so much beauty can be found in one sheet of paper. Here are a few patterns to try out. They would be beautiful tacked to a wall, used in a book, or wrapped around a lamp (see page 46). Refer to page 19 for a refresher on mountain, valley, and universal folds.

HOW TO USE WHITE

The subtlety and cleanliness of an all-white palette enhances the shadows created by the precise folding.

MATERIALS

templates (page 176–78)
paper
bone folder

COLORS

monochromatic whites

TIME

a few episodes of
The Great British Bake Off

INSPIRATION

architectural elements

(INSTRUCTIONS)

A

FOLDING TECHNIQUE: REPEATED CHEVRON

1 If using the template, print at 200 percent on the wrong side of the paper.

2 Accordion fold as many vertical lines as you'd like. (If using the template, make universal folds by creasing each fold in both a mountain and valley direction along all the vertical lines of the template.)

3 A systematic method for doing this is to fold your paper in half vertically. Open the paper and then fold each half in half. Open the paper again, and then continue to fold each half in half until you have made the appropriate number of creases. When you are finished, you should be able to accordion fold the entire sheet into something the width of half of one chevron.

4 Sharply crease the folds.

5 With all your vertical folds collapsed in an accordion, make universal creases along all the diagonal lines to create guides.

6 Unfold the paper, and sharply crease along the guides.

7 Manipulate the paper so the folds match those in the template.

B

FOLDING TECHNIQUE: ARROWHEAD

1 If using the template, print at 200 percent on the wrong side of the paper.

2 Mountain fold the paper in half diagonally.

3 Orient the folded paper so it forms a right angle with the straight edges on the left and on the bottom.

4 Universally fold this triangle in half vertically (so the fold is parallel to the left edge of the triangle). Unfold and universally fold each of the halves in half again (so there are three vertical folds parallel to the left edge of the triangle). Unfold and universally fold each of these halves one more time.

5 Unfold and manipulate the paper so all the folds match those on the template.

C

FOLDING TECHNIQUE: SQUARE

1 If using the template, print at 200 percent on the wrong side of the paper.

2 Valley fold the paper in half horizontally.

3 Valley fold the paper in half vertically.

4 Universal fold the paper in half diagonally in both directions.

5 Follow the directions for Folding Technique: Arrowhead for each quadrant.

FOLDING TECHNIQUE: CYLINDER (NOT SHOWN)

1 If using the template, print at 200 percent on the wrong side of the paper.

2 Accordion fold as many vertical lines as you'd like. (If using the template, make universal folds by creasing each fold in both a mountain and valley direction, along all the vertical lines of the template.)

3 A systematic method for doing this is to fold your paper in half vertically. Open the paper and fold each half in half. Open the paper again, and then continue to fold each half in half until you have made the appropriate number of creases. When you are finished, you should be able to accordion fold the entire sheet into something the width of half of one diamond.

4 Sharply crease these folds.

5 Mountain fold along all the diagonal lines.

6 Manipulate the paper so the folds match those in the template. As the folds start to take shape, a cylinder will form. When completely collapsed accordion style, the folds will form the letter C.

HOLLY-AND-BERRY GARLAND

My mom is the most creative person I know, but for the holidays, when my sister and I come home to visit, she gives us free rein to craft our hearts out. You can imagine the joy this brings to someone who does it for a living. One year she wanted something to adorn the staircase, so we came up with a holly-and-berry paper garland. I shared it on the blog the following year, and it was a hit! Readers have been sharing their own holly-and-berry garlands online, and I'm so tickled each time I see one. We like to try something different year after year, and the beauty of paper decorations is that they are recyclable. However, if you take care of them properly, you can also keep and reuse them.

HOW TO USE WHITE

The original garland was a classic green-and-red combination, but I thought it would be elegant in an all-white scheme to lend a wintry effect. I used an off-white with more yellow instead of a blue-white, which feels colder. I finished it off with some gold berries. Gold always adds a touch of class.

COLORS

white and gold

TIME

a crafternoon with family
listening to holiday tunes

INSPIRATION

holly and berries

(MATERIALS)

template (page 179)

white paper

scissors

pencil

seamless 26-inch-wide (66-cm)
    photography paper roll

bone folder

paper cutter

gold paper (or white paper
    spray-painted gold)

glue gun

brown painter's paper

masking tape

chenille floral wire

(INSTRUCTIONS)

Ⓐ
LEAVES

1 Copy the template onto white paper, and cut out. Trace onto the photography roll, and cut out enough leaves to fill the installation space. Count on 2 leaves per foot. Score the middle of each leaf with a bone folder.

Ⓑ
BERRIES

1 Using the paper cutter, cut 1-inch (2.5-cm) strips of the gold paper, four per berry.

2 Make a loop and glue together the ends.

3 Make another loop and wrap around the first, going in the opposite direction. Glue together the ends.

4 Repeat with the last two strips to form a berry.

Ⓒ
GARLAND

1 Twist the painter's paper to form a rope shape, and secure with tape. Glue holly leaves to the rope, switching directions at every other leaf. Glue on the berries. Use chenille floral wire to secure garland to the banister.

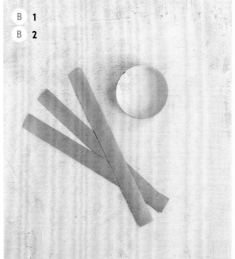

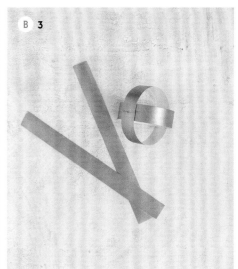

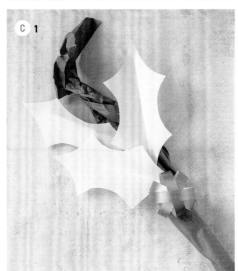

PAPER MARBLING

My great-grandmother Marilla Zatelle was a six-foot-tall proud Danish woman who gabbed about family history the way most people chat about the weather. She kept intricate records with carefully labeled photos. My grandmother Dorothy carried on the tradition, and every visit included a look through our photos and an introduction to relatives I would never meet. To this day, I can name family members many generations back and identify individual penmanship. For this project, I wanted to capture the beauty and nostalgia of old family photos by creating a classic black-and-white stationery, and paper marbling was the perfect way to do so.

Paper marbling is a traditional Japanese method of applying ink on water to paper. Part of the appeal is that no two prints are alike, which allows you to play and have fun with the process. This method doesn't come with the instructions on a marbling kit, so you have more control over your designs. Go wild!

HOW TO USE WHITE

Black is to white as mustard is to ketchup—a classic, no-fail combination. Here, we create a timeless quality using off-white paper and a lighter-value black (aka gray).

COLORS

black and white

TIME

a crafternoon with friends listening to a '90s playlist

INSPIRATION

old family photos

(MATERIALS)

- newspaper or a towel
- photography tray (a cake pan also works well)
- water
- small containers (the plastic condiment cups with lids that you can get in a package at the grocery store work well)
- dispersant or surfactant (marbling kits come with one, or you can use dishwashing liquid, Kodak Photo-Flo, or ox gall liquid—you need only one)
- Japanese or Chinese writing ink or a Suminagachi marbling kit (easy to find at art-supply stores or online)
- paintbrushes (inexpensive watercolor brushes work just fine)
- barbecue or bamboo skewers
- medium-weight absorbent non-coated papers (smaller than the size of your tray)

(INSTRUCTIONS)

1 Set aside newspaper or a towel. Fill the tray with a few inches of water. Pour a little bit of water into a small container. Add one or two drops of the dispersant. This will be your white. Add a few squirts of black ink to a second small container. (If you want to work with colored ink instead, use a separate container for each color.)

2 Dip a paintbrush in a color, and then carefully touch your brush to the very top of the water in the tray. The color will spread on top of the water. If you push the brush too far into the water, the ink will sink to the bottom and/or muddy the water. If this happens, start over.

3 Dip another brush into the dispersant water or a new color and place the brush in the ink floating on the water. Alternate color and dispersant water to create a series of rings. The ink is often light at first, but gets more saturated as it moves to the perimeter of the tray.

4 Use a skewer to carefully move through the design in the water, creating a swirling pattern.

5 When your design is complete, carefully pick up the paper by lifting from one side with your fingers, and set it on the top of the water.

6 Leave it in for a couple of seconds before taking it out of the water with fingers on opposite ends. Lay the paper face up on the newspaper or towel. Let dry.

TIPS:

* If the ink or dispersant water spreads too quickly or too far, you have used too much dispersant. If the ink doesn't spread, add more dispersant.

* If the ink appears runny when you pull your paper out of the water, rinse the paper quickly under the tap.

"Every color is my favorite color. I'm passionate about all colors, colors of the rainbow, colors that are blended and mixed."

—NATALIE MILLER, *fiber artist*

Brides typically have set colors for their weddings. Usually it's one or two, three if you're indecisive. When planning my wedding, I started with a deep rose pink. As I began working with it, I couldn't help but add a light pink because I love monochromatics; and then, of course, peach, which works so well with pinks; then chartreuse, off-white, deep olive green, bright lemon yellow. Before I knew it, every color of the RAINBOW *was represented in my palette. I feel that colors need each other. It's one of the reasons you'll find so much color in my work. I can't resist the full color spectrum.*

The phenomenon of the rainbow is nature's way of showing us how to use the color wheel. Red bleeds to orange, which merges into yellow, then green, blue, indigo, and then finally violet. This chapter is all about using the colors of the **RAINBOW** *to create beautiful crafts. Hint: You don't always need every color of the* RAINBOW *to make it feel complete.*

FUN FACTS ABOUT RAINBOW:

→ IN GREEK AND ROMAN TIMES, IT WAS BELIEVED THAT THE GODDESS IRIS CREATED THE RAINBOW AS A PATH LINKING US TO THE IMMORTALS. → IN 1637, RENÉ DESCARTES DISCOVERED THAT RAINBOWS WERE THE RESULT OF RAINDROPS CREATING PRISMS THAT SPLIT LIGHT FROM THE SUN INTO DIFFERENT COLORS. GOLD STAR FOR DESCARTES. → RAINBOWS CAN EXIST AT NIGHT. WHEN LIGHT FROM THE MOON DISPERSES THROUGH WATER DROPLETS, THE RESULT IS KNOWN AS A MOONBOW. BECAUSE MOONLIGHT IS FAINTER THAN SUNLIGHT, THE BOW ITSELF MAY APPEAR WHITE, BUT A LONG-EXPOSURE CAMERA CAN CAPTURE THE FULL ARRAY OF COLORS.

PAPIER-MÂCHÉ CAKE STANDS

Both my grandfathers were dentists, so while growing up I learned the importance of good dental hygiene. But what child can refuse the temptation of a strategically placed gumball machine? It requires only a quarter yet dispenses happiness equal to a tax refund. Gumballs are so big and juicy and colorful. Which color is going to pop out? And who are you going to have to trade with to get the blue one? It's all such a mystery!

These papier-mâché cake stands recall the classic gumball, but they are intended to hold a favorite dessert. Have fun creating unique formations.

HOW TO USE RAINBOW

I created five cake stands to complete the rainbow, but if you're just making one, consider painting the stand in all the rainbow colors. I used monochromatic shades for each hue, leaving out purple. For orange, I employed a coral-peach, and I also combined pink and red.

COLORS

rainbow

TIME

watching *Les Demoiselles de Rochefort*
(the colors will inspire!)
(and 24 to 72 hours for drying . . .)

INSPIRATION

gumballs

(**MATERIALS**)

Styrofoam shapes (disks, balls, cones)

knife

glue gun

5-gallon (20-L) bucket or deep bowl

water

flour

newspaper

house paint or high-gloss acrylic paint

foam paintbrushes

(INSTRUCTIONS)

1   For each cake stand you will need one Styrofoam disk and a combination of balls and cones. For some I used just one ball or cone, and for others I used multiple pieces.

2   Use a knife to level off the surfaces of the round objects so they lie flush.

3   Glue the pieces together to form the cake stand: you can use whatever pattern you like (see the photo for ideas).

4   In the bucket, mix one part water with one part flour to create your papier-mâché mixture. Start with 1 cup of each, and make more as needed.

5   Tear the newspaper into thin strips.

6   Dip the strips into the papier-mâché mixture and begin to cover the cake stand. Make sure the pieces are as smooth as possible. When the cake stand is covered, let dry 24 hours.

7   Apply one or two more layers of papier-mâché to ensure you have a smooth, even surface. Let each layer dry completely before applying another.

8   Paint each shape in coordinating colors.

TIP: *When using the cake stand, place a piece of parchment paper between food and surface to keep the stand clean.*

IKEBANA FLORAL ARRANGEMENT

I f you love the look and feel of wildflowers but sometimes crave a more orderly arrangement, you may be intrigued by *ikebana*. The Japanese are masters of order, and ikebana is the perfect way to incorporate organization and restraint into the chaos of nature. This is the disciplined art of arranging flowers, and it follows a strict set of rules concerning color, shape, and line. I wanted to include as many colors of the rainbow as possible but still maintain a cohesive, restrained look, and ikebana was the perfect way to achieve that. I created an ikebana arrangement with paper Japanese anemones and whimsical colorful daisies. Have fun experimenting with different forms and shapes, and let them inform your design.

HOW TO USE RAINBOW

I used desaturated colors to achieve a beautiful, more realistic floral palette. Every color of the rainbow is represented by paper selection and paint. Think deep red, blue-gray, mustard yellow, red-orange, indigo, plum, and olive green.

COLORS

a desaturated rainbow

TIME

bingeing on *Seinfeld*

INSPIRATION

Japanese ikebana

(MATERIALS)

templates (pages 180–81)

white paper

scissors

pencil

pastel paper in every shade

glue gun

5 18-inch (46-cm) 22-gauge cloth-covered wires

watercolors or gouache (optional)

paintbrush (optional)

standard hole punch

yellow tissue or crepe paper

⅜-inch (1-cm) cotton ball

chartreuse fine crepe paper

wire cutters

1/16-inch (1.5-mm) hole punch

floral frog

vessel

floral foam

moss

(INSTRUCTIONS)

LEAVES

1 Copy the templates onto white paper, and cut out. Trace onto green pastel paper, and cut out. Paint details with gouache or watercolor, if desired.

2 Curl the leaves by pulling them over your finger, a paintbrush handle, or a pencil.

3 Glue the base of the leaves onto a piece of wire, alternating sides around the wire. Start with the smallest leaf at the top and continue to the bottom.

JAPANESE ANEMONE

1 Copy the templates onto white paper, and cut out. Trace onto pastel paper, and cut out three petals per flower.

2 Use the standard punch to make a hole in the middle of each petal. Use a pencil or a paintbrush handle to curl one side of the petal edge up and the other side down.

3 Cut out two circles of yellow tissue or crepe paper per flower, one 1 inch (2.5 cm) and the other 1½ inches (4 cm). Cut fringe into the circle all the way around. Gently roll each piece of fringe for better texture.

4 Glue a cotton ball to the top of a wire. Cut a 2-inch (5-cm) piece of chartreuse fine crepe paper and wrap it over the cotton ball like a lollipop wrapper. Glue in place and cut off any extra (A).

5 Slide the two yellow fringed circles onto the wire (B). Next, slide the three petals onto the wire, and spread evenly around the center. Glue to secure on the bottom (C).

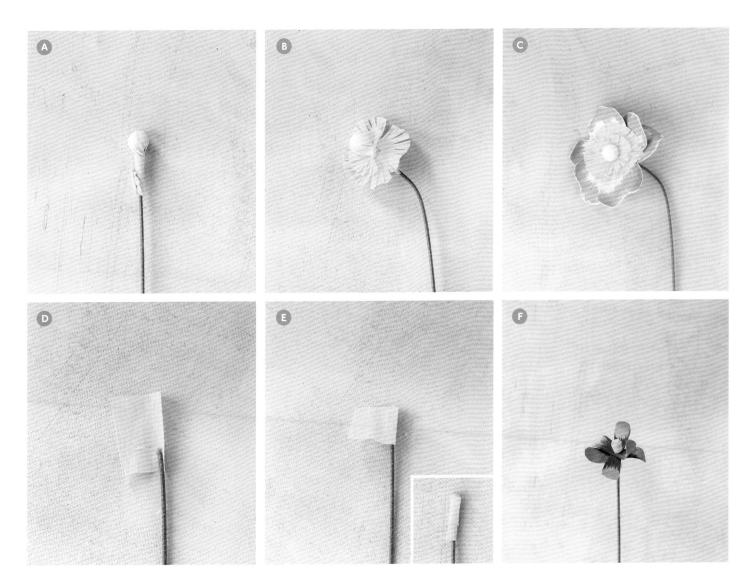

SMALL FLOWER

1   Copy the templates onto white paper, and cut out. Trace onto pastel paper, and cut out three petals. Paint details with gouache or watercolor, if desired.

2   Cut out a ¾ by ½-inch (2 by 1.3-cm) strip of yellow tissue or crepe paper.

3   Cut a piece of wire to 8 inches. Glue wire halfway up the tissue paper on the far right (D).

4   Fold the paper over and glue in place. This will be the center of the flower. Roll up the paper like a snail and glue in place (E).

5   Use the ¹⁄₁₆-inch (1.5-mm) punch to make a hole in the center of each petal.

6   Slide the petals on the wire to the yellow centers and secure with glue (F).

CREATING THE ARRANGEMENT

1   Put a floral frog in the base of your vessel and top with a piece of floral foam that is slightly smaller than your vessel.

2   Stick your flowers and foliage into the foam and arrange to your satisfaction. Add moss on top to cover the foam (see page 120).

CREPE PAPER STREAMERS

On our birthdays, my siblings and I would scurry downstairs to find a surprise of banners, garlands, or balloons—all courtesy of our mom, who worked like one of Santa's elves during the night. Each time, the house was decorated differently. With four kids, that's a lot of birthday decorating! One memorable year she hung streamers in every shade of the rainbow vertically rather than corner to corner. This created an ethereal dream that I have yet to forget. Crepe paper streamers are such a quick and easy way to decorate. Keep them on hand for a last-minute party idea. They are perfect for birthday twirling.

HOW TO USE RAINBOW

The dollar store carries multiple shades of crepe paper streamers in every color: hot pink, light pink, red, dark red, orange, peach, golden yellow, light yellow, lime green, dark green, mint green, teal, light blue, dark blue, lavender, grape purple, white, black, gray. Go crazy with color! If you want more subtle tone variations, try ordering the same color from a few different companies

COLORS

rainbow

TIME

headphones in,
one Michael Jackson album

INSPIRATION

childhood birthday parties

(MATERIALS)

crepe paper party streamers in
   rainbow colors

masking tape or sticky tack

scissors

(INSTRUCTIONS)

Arrange the streamers in rainbow order. Affix them to the ceiling, doorway, or a chosen location. Secure only the top of the streamer so the rest falls gently and hangs free. Trim any streamers as desired.

COLOR WHEEL TABLECLOTH

The Mad Tea Party in *Alice in Wonderland* will forever be one of my favorite sources of inspiration. The scene creates sensory overload: the colors, the food, the guests—it's mesmerizing. I wanted to create an equally magical, but a bit more polished, experience for a party. The color wheel was a perfect way to include a rainbow of colors in a cohesive manner. I used color-coordinated paper goods to increase the whimsical feel. More is more in this case, so go to town with all the party supplies and make those Mad Hatters proud!

HOW TO USE RAINBOW

I created a full rainbow by giving each color wedge about two shades each (three for blue). You can add or delete the amount of colors depending on the number of guests.

COLORS

full rainbow

TIME

watching *Amélie*

INSPIRATION

color wheel

(MATERIALS)

large cardstock sheets in rainbow colors (for a less-expensive option, paint butcher paper)

scissors

ruler

(INSTRUCTIONS)

1   A bit of math is required if you want the wedges spread evenly throughout the circle. If you're not concerned about being exact, eyeball the widths of the wedges and trace to the shape of the round table.

Formula:
Arc length = $2\pi R*(C/360)$

C = number of desired color wedges

R = Radius of your table (diameter of the table/2)

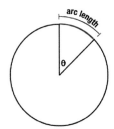

2   Cut out the first wedge and use as a template to cut out desired number of wedges.

3   Arrange the wedges in your preferred order.

RAINBOW NECKLACE

The rainbow became a common motif during the rise of the counterculture of the 1960s and '70s with its groovy emphasis on peace, love, and freedom. The rainbows of the time captured the characteristic color palettes of the era with mustard yellow, burnt orange, red, purple, and blue; green was frequently omitted. I wanted to create a piece of jewelry that used the colors of the rainbow but didn't have the in-your-face quality of the common motif. This muted palette was the way to go.

HOW TO USE RAINBOW

Muted 1960s-era rainbow, minus green. The rainbow is toned down with two variations on gray so you can easily weave it into your wardrobe. Consider it a more sophisticated rainbow.

COLORS

muted rainbow, minus green

TIME

an episode of *Gilmore Girls*

INSPIRATION

shoe tassels

(MATERIALS)

cardstock in six colors of the rainbow and two shades of gray

fringe scissors

scissors

glue gun

white paper

pencil

templates (page 181)

glue stick

silver bail (jewelry notion)

thin silver necklace chain

(INSTRUCTIONS)

1 From the six colors of cardstock, cut 1½ by 7-inch (4 by 18-cm) sheets and fringe each one.

2 Tightly roll each fringed sheet so the fringe faces downward and creates a small tassel as shown. Secure with a dot of glue.

3 Copy the templates onto white paper, and cut out. Trace onto gray cardstock, and cut out.

4 Use the glue gun to affix the six tassels to one large semicircle shape.

5 With a glue stick, adhere the small semicircle to the other large semicircle, and then glue on top of the tassels, sandwiching the tassels between the two large semi-circles.

6 Glue the silver bail onto the top of the bottom semi-circle so it sticks out on top for the necklace chain to slip through.

7 Glue the thin gray piece of paper along the top to enclose the tassels. Slip the chain through the bail.

RAINBOW ORIGAMI BOOK

spotted this origami technique when I interned at the National Museum of Women in the Arts in Washington, D.C., during college. There was a book art exhibition going on, and the books were wildly inventive. This medium was new to me, and it seemed simple even though the artist's application was much more involved. Here, I crafted a book to showcase a bright and saturated rainbow. Once you've created your book, start filling it in with mini photos, notes, ticket stubs, stickers, and the like. Refer to page 19 for a refresher on mountain, valley, and universal folds.

HOW TO USE RAINBOW

I used a complete rainbow with two shades for every hue. Feel free to select as many shades as you like—the more shades, the longer the book. Origami paper has some of the most beautiful colors, so it will be hard to choose!

COLORS

complete color wheel rainbow

TIME

an episode of *The Crown*

INSPIRATION

rainbow arc

(MATERIALS)

templates (page 182–83)

origami paper in as many colors as you'd like

bone folder

glue stick

ribbon (optional)

cardstock (optional)

1   Copy the template onto the back of sheets of origami paper so it's hidden when the book is complete.

2   The primary pages will be displayed in their entirety when the book is opened and the pages are unfolded. The secondary pages connect the primary pages. When the book is opened and the pages are unfolded, you will see just two corners of the secondary pages.

3   Lay out the sheets of origami paper in your preferred order, colored side up. Begin with a primary page on top, alternate every other page with a secondary page, and then end with a primary page on the bottom.

4   Fold all the primary pages, creasing sharply, as follows:

With the back side up (the non-colored side with the template if you've printed out the template), mountain fold the paper vertically in half. Mountain fold the paper horizontally in half (A).

Valley fold the paper diagonally in half (B).

Open the valley fold. Flip the paper over (front or color side up). Push the middle of the paper where all the folds intersect down and then push the two quadrants with folds down their middle in until those folds meet (C).

5   Fold all the secondary pages, creasing each fold sharply, as follows:

With the back side up (the non-colored side with the template if you've printed out the template), valley fold the paper vertically in half.

Valley fold the paper horizontally in half.

Mountain fold the paper diagonally in half.

As before, open the valley fold. Flip the paper over. Push the center down while pushing in the quadrants with the folds.

6   Lay out all the pages (both primary and secondary) with the diagonal folds oriented so they form vertical parallel lines with a paper point at the top and a paper point at the bottom. Make sure the left and right corners of the primary pages completely overlap the left and right corners of the secondary pages. (The right corner of Page 1 should meet the left corner of Page 3, overlapping Page 2.)

7   Glue the back of the primary page to the front of the secondary page where the two pages overlap (D).

8   When finished gluing, fold up the book along the folds already created. (The finished book should be one quarter the size of the starting sheet of paper.)

Optional: Glue one ribbon to the outside of the front cover and one ribbon to the outside of the back cover. Create two covers out of cardstock that is slightly bigger than the finished folded square and glue them over the ribbons. Tie the ribbons to hold the book shut.

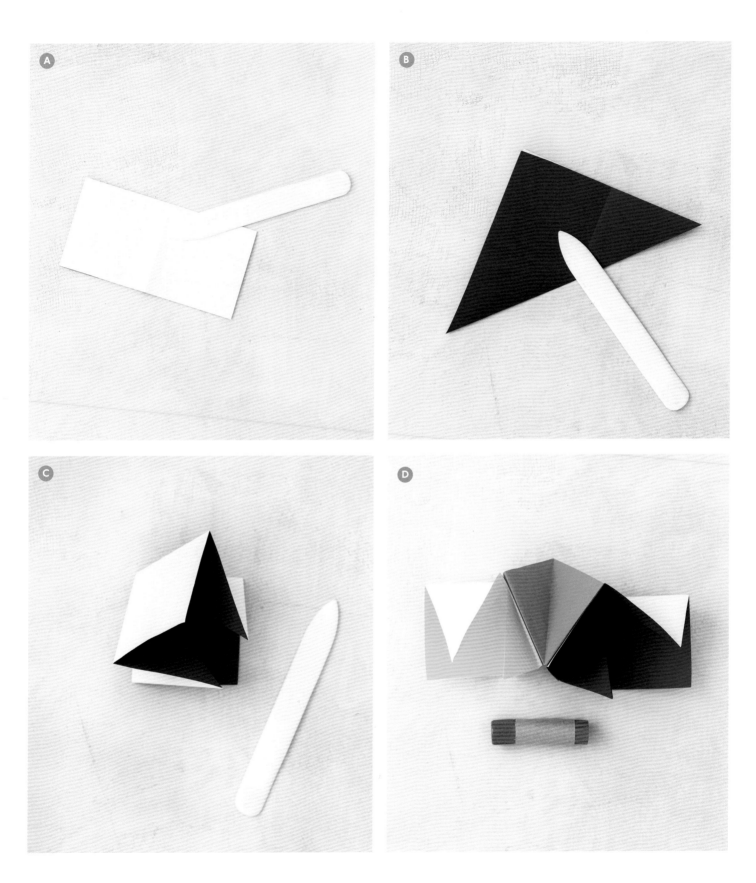

When you were in grade school, your teacher may have taught you how to make oversize Easter eggs (as mine did) by papier-mâché-ing a balloon and covering it with cutout squares of tissue paper applied with the tip of a pencil. I have such a wonderful memory of the day I selected my colors and created my decorative patterns. I've always thought the technique would be stellar for something more involved. Enter the boucherouite rug. Traditionally, these antique Moroccan rugs were created with bits of leftover textiles when raw materials were harder to come by. These rugs are generally created in bright colors with wild patterns, and because they're made from scraps they have a lot of imperfections. The tissue paper process lends itself to a similar aesthetic.

Although the technique is quite simple, making the rug can be time-consuming, depending on how full you want it to be. There are additional designs available on *The House That Lars Built* for those who are looking for a quicker project.

HOW TO USE RAINBOW

I used every color of the rainbow, plus white, black, and gray. Tissue paper comes in rainbow packs with in-between shades that are perfect for making rugs. Have fun mixing up the colors, but I recommend staying with similar tones. I've included my color recommendations here, but feel free to experiment!

COLORS

every shade of the rainbow

TIME

a season of *The Bachelor*

INSPIRATION

Boucherouite Moroccan rug

(MATERIALS)

template*

rainbow pack of tissue paper

50-pack tissue paper of each in hot pink, red, black, white, yellow

100-pack tissue paper in natural white

rotary cutter and mat or scissors

pencil or straw to facilitate gluing

white glue

* www.crafttherainbow.com/booktemplates

(INSTRUCTIONS)

1 Print the template at a copy shop as a black-and-white engineer print. (This should cost just a few dollars.)

2 Use the color guide to match the tissue paper to its placement on the template.

3 Cut 2 by 2-inch (5 by 5-cm) squares of tissue paper in all the colors with your rotary cutter and mat or scissors.

4 Wrap a tissue square around the eraser edge of a pencil or a straw.

5 Dip the edge of the tissue paper into some glue and place on the rug template.

6 Glue the tissue paper squares as close together as possible for a full look. Place further apart for a less-full look.

TIP: *Adhere to a wall with adhesive strips for framing or wrap around a dowel at the top and use string.*

HANDMADE TERRAZZO PAPER

ere's another grade-school technique that is just as much fun when updated. I was inspired by terrazzo tile and its bits of marble, quartz, granite, and glass. Handmade paper has such a wonderfully rich texture, and you can use it for notes, bunting, gift tags—you name it!

HOW TO USE RAINBOW

I wanted the rainbow here to feel more mid-twentieth-century, so I kept many of the bright hues and added colors like sage green, baby pink, and light blue. Black added a more sophisticated vibe. Think Ray and Charles Eames!

COLORS

saturated rainbow with a few wild cards

TIME

watching *Little Women*

INSPIRATION

terrazzo tile and stones

(MATERIALS)

6 to 8 scraps of white office paper

scissors

colored scraps from other projects

blender

water

large, shallow container, like an aluminum disposable pan or shallow tub

2 screen splatter guards, one slightly larger than the other

dry dish towel

sponge

(INSTRUCTIONS)

1 Cut white scraps into 1 by 5-inch (2.5 by 13-cm) strips.

2 Cut colored scraps into small geometric shapes.

3 Put white strips in a blender and cover with water. Let soak for about 15 minutes.

4 Blend paper and water until frothy.

5 Fill the shallow container with 1 to 2 inches (2.5 to 5-cm) of water.

6 Pour blended paper into the container. Spread mixture around the entire pan.

7 Dip the smaller splatter guard into the mixture, making sure to hold it level. Lightly shake until the entire screen is covered.

8 Holding the splatter guard level, pull it out. (It may take a couple of dips to get it covered just right.)

9 Place the covered splatter guard on a dry dish towel.

10 Place the larger splatter guard on top of the covered one and lightly press a sponge against it to soak up excess water. Remove splatter guard and add colored pieces on top. Let dry.

TIP: *If you want the paper to feel more layered, you can add the colored pieces into the container with the blended white office paper. However, they will be brighter if you add them in afterward.*

POM-POM BASKETS

Organization is not my forte, but when I have lovely containers in which to put things I am much more likely to pick up after myself. Or at least that's what I tell myself. I dream of a future mudroom for collecting the bits and bobs that end up strewn around the house in these rainbow baskets. The simple, collapsible shape is perfect when not in use, but dressed to the nines in colorful poms, you won't want to hide them for long

HOW TO USE RAINBOW

I chose one basket for each color group (except purple), then painted the bottom of the basket in a pastel of the color. The poms feature an analogous trio of colors: light pink, dark pink, bright pink; yellow, orange, gold; light blue, dark blue, medium blue; mint, dark green, sage; off-white, silver, gray.

(MATERIALS)

crepe paper in rainbow shades
scissors
fringe scissors
glue gun
house or acrylic paint
paintbrush
woven seagrass baskets

COLORS

rainbow

TIME

an episode of *Stuff You Should Know*

INSPIRATION

traditional African baskets

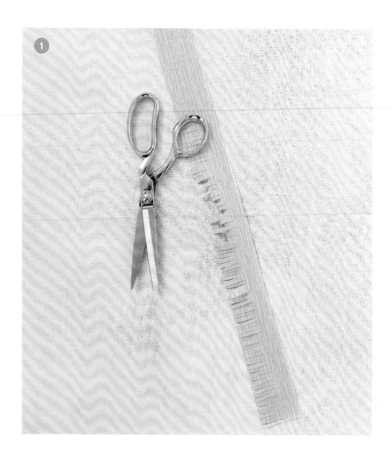

(INSTRUCTIONS)

1 Cut crepe paper into 1½ by 24-inch (4 by 61-cm) pieces (larger if you want thicker pom-poms). Fringe the long edge of your crepe paper, leaving a ¼-inch (6-mm) border along the top.

2 Begin rolling up the fringed piece tightly, fluffing the fringed edges outward as you roll.

3 When you get to the end, glue the edge. Repeat for as many pom-poms as desired.

4 Paint the bottom of the basket in a color that coordinates with the pom-poms. Let dry.

5 Glue the poms onto the top of the basket.

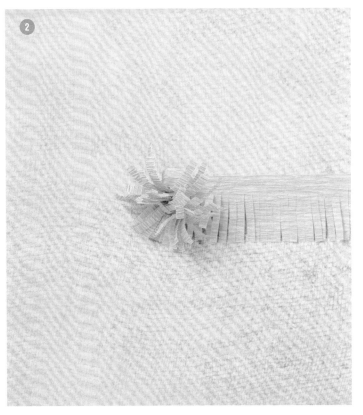

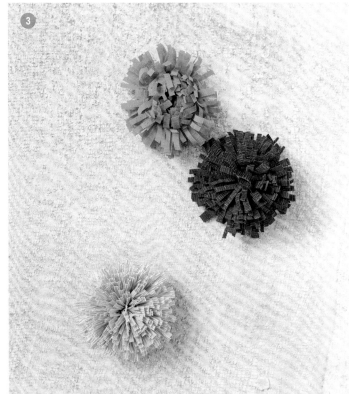

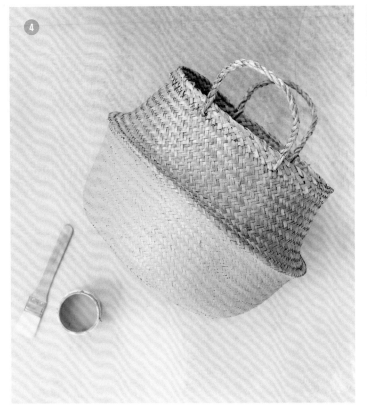

RAINBOW PAPER PLANTS

Sadly, we are not all blessed with a green thumb, no matter how many times a coworker gives us a potted orchid—I've killed too many to mention. A garden of paper plants is my current strategy for boosting morale and keeping my spirits high. Making your own paper plants also means you are not confined to a strict green color palette. Rainbow paper houseplants will put your ficus tree to shame!

HOW TO USE RAINBOW

I replaced a bright red with a light pink, but otherwise every color of the rainbow is represented and pretty glasses enhance the play of light and color.

COLORS

pink, orange, yellow,
green, blue, purple

TIME

one VHS of *Anne of Green Gables*

INSPIRATION

colorful floral painting

(MATERIALS)

templates (page 184–85)

white paper

scissors

180-gram crepe paper in pink,
coral, yellow, purple, and blue

pencil

10 18-inch (46-cm) 18-gauge
cloth-covered wires

wire cutters

glue gun

marbled paper in green, coral,
purple, and blue

craft knife

(INSTRUCTIONS)

Ⓐ

PINK PLANT

1 Copy the templates onto white paper, and cut out. Place the templates on the diagonal of pink crepe paper so the grain creates a V pattern in the leaf. Trace and cut out.

2 Cut three to five thin strips of pink crepe paper against the grain, gently stretch them out, and wrap them around two wires.

3 Cut one wire into three 6-inch (15-cm) pieces.

4 Glue a leaf onto the end of each 6-inch (15-cm) piece of wire.

5 Group the leaves together with the remaining wire, and wrap with another strip of crepe paper to create one bough. Gently bend the leaves to give them some shape.

Ⓑ

BLUE PLANT

1 Copy the template onto white paper, and cut out. Trace onto blue marbled paper, and cut out.

2 Cut one to three thin strips of blue crepe paper, stretch them out, and wrap them around a wire.

3 Glue the leaf onto the wire. Gently bend the leaf to give it some shape.

Ⓒ

ORANGE PLANT

1 Copy the templates onto white paper, and cut out. Trace onto orange marbled paper, and cut out.

2 Score each leaf with a craft knife.

3 Cut one to three thin strips of coral crepe paper against the grain, gently stretch them out, and wrap them around one wire.

4 Glue the leaves onto the wire. Gently bend the leaves to give them some shape.

Ⓓ

PURPLE PLANT

1 Copy the template onto white paper, and cut out. Trace onto purple marbled paper, and cut out.

2 Cut out three to five thin strips of crepe paper against the grain, gently stretch them out, and wrap them around three wires.

3 Glue a leaf onto each wire, making sure the wire goes to the tip of the leaf. Gently bend the leaves to give them some shape. Arrange leaves as desired.

Ⓔ

GREEN PLANT

1 Copy the template onto white paper, and cut out. Trace onto green marbled paper, and cut out.

2 Cut three to five thin strips of yellow crepe paper against the grain, gently stretch them out, and wrap them around three wires.

3 Glue a leaf onto the end of each wire.

4 Stagger the leaves, group together, and wrap with another strip of crepe paper to create one bough. Gently bend the leaves to give them some shape.

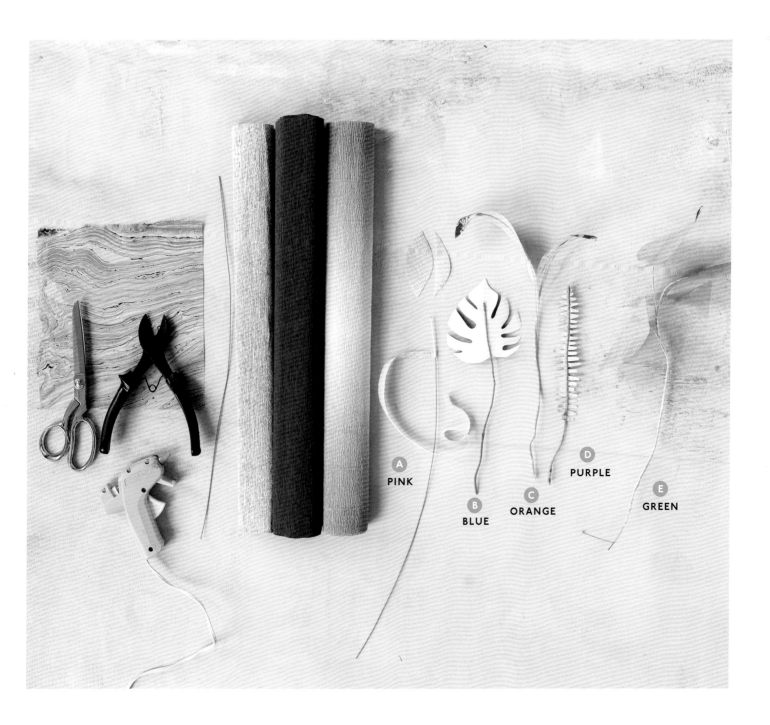

A PINK

B BLUE

C ORANGE

D PURPLE

E GREEN

FLOWER CROWN

After living in one of the most northern countries in the world, where winter light appears at 9 A.M. and disappears at 3:30 in the afternoon, this California girl has developed a new appreciation for the sun. I adored it before, and I love it even more now. I also understand why one of the biggest Scandinavian holidays is Midsummer, a celebration of the longest day of the year in June. In Sweden, they adorn themselves with floral crowns, raise a maypole, and dance around. When I returned to the United States, I continued the celebration and adopted these Swedish traditions to remind myself of the beauty of the non-winter season.

This flower crown features tiny flowers in small groupings that are light and airy, like a lovely summer day. You can use it for a special celebration, for décor, or just for fun. Feel free to add in your own favorite summer blooms.

HOW TO USE RAINBOW

I used coral red, peach, yellow-green, light blue, and orchid purple with accents of white to feel like a Swedish meadow. Pick a palette that reminds you of your favorite outdoor spot. I left out green and replaced it with metallic champagne to remind me of the glimmering summer nights of Scandinavia.

COLORS

rainbow

TIME

the old *Pride and Prejudice*

INSPIRATION

Scandinavian Midsummer floral crown

(MATERIALS)

double-sided 90-gram crepe paper, 160-gram crepe paper, and/or 180-gram crepe paper in blues, lilac, pinks, coral, yellow, and metallic gold

scissors

fringe scissors

glue gun

12 22-gauge cloth-covered wires, cut into 2-inch (5-cm) lengths

wire cutters

3 to 5 ⅜-inch (1-cm) cotton balls

acrylic paints

small paintbrushes

templates (page 186)

white paper

pencil

2 18-inch (46 cm) 18-gauge paper-covered wires

FLOWER CENTERS

1 There are three different techniques for flower centers: the fringed center, the cotton spun ball center, and the paper-covered center.

2 For the fringed center, cut a ½ by 1-inch (1.3 by 2.5-cm) piece of crepe paper. Fringe along one edge and roll tightly together. Glue to the tip of a piece of cloth-covered wire.

3 For the cotton spun ball center, paint the cotton ball in your desired color and let dry. Glue to the tip of a piece of cloth-covered wire.

4 For the paper-covered center, see Ikebana Small Flower instructions 2 to 4 on page 123.

BELL-SHAPED FLOWERS

1 Copy the template onto white paper, and cut out. Trace bell onto crepe paper, and cut out. Gently stretch out the paper (A).

2 Roll the flower, and glue the edges together (B).

3 On the non-wavy edge, glue a piece of cloth-covered wire about ¼ inch (6 mm) inside the flower and squeeze to secure (C).

4 Use the eraser end of a pencil or your forefinger to gently push out the bottom to create the bell shape (D).

5 Cut a ¼ by 5-inch (6 mm by 12-cm) strip of crepe paper against the grain, and gently stretch it out.

6 Glue the edge of the strip to the top of the wire and wrap it around. Secure with glue at the end (E).

PETAL-BASED FLOWERS

1 Copy the templates onto white paper, and cut out. Trace onto crepe paper, and cut out three to eight petals of the same shape for each flower (G).

2 Add a dab of glue at the base of a petal and adhere the petal to a piece of cloth-covered wire. Repeat with remaining petals, spacing evenly (H).

3 Wrap the stem in the same way as for the bell-shaped flower (I).

TIP: *Add some dimension by painting the base or the tip of each petal with a coordinating shade of paint. (I like to use monochromatic colors; I put light paint on dark petals and dark paint on light petals.)*

LEAVES

1 Copy the template onto white paper, and cut out. Trace onto crepe paper, and cut out. Curl the leaves (see Ikebana Floral Arrangements, page 120).

2 Make clusters of leaves by gluing one leaf to a 2-inch (5-cm) piece of cloth-covered wire (F), then wrap crepe paper around the stem about ½ inch (1.3 cm) down. Add in another leaf that has been attached to a stem and continue wrapping around the main stem with crepe paper. Repeat until you have three to four leaves per cluster.

MAKING THE CROWN

1 Shape the paper-covered wires into a circle that fits around your head, and wrap the ends of the wire together. Bend back the ends so you can use them as hooks to secure the crown to your head. Wrap the wire with gold crepe paper.

2 Wrap the flowers around the crown. Start at the center front, and work your way around each side to the back.

3 Glue leaves onto the flowers, one to two per flower, and add leaf clusters, spacing evenly throughout.

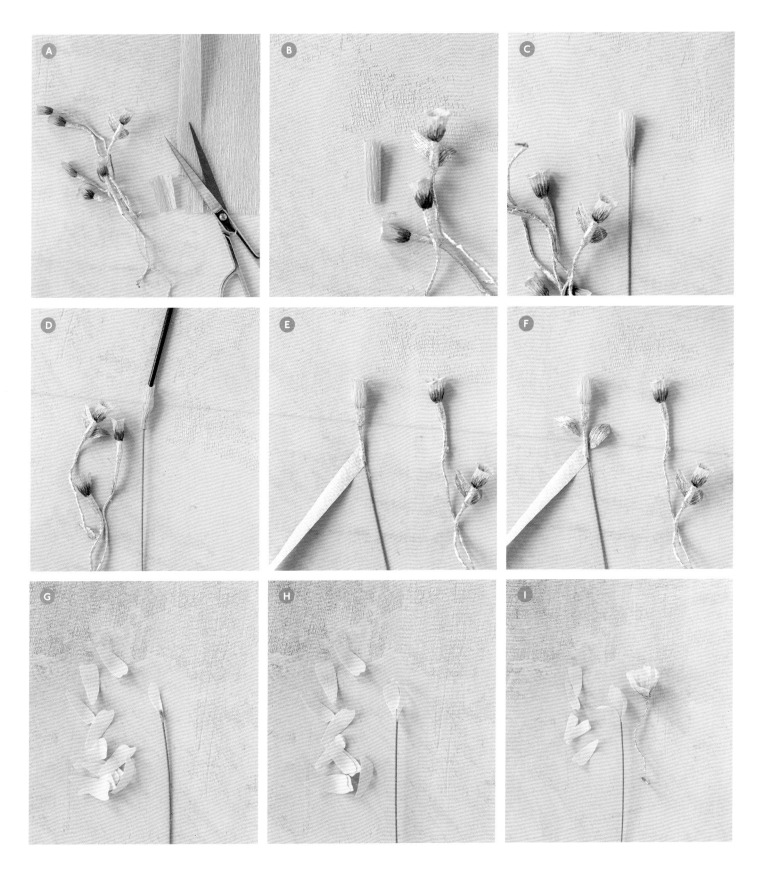

RAINBOW HONEYCOMB

If you're like me, you have a genuine affinity for honeybees, particularly the vintage motifs you see on posters or apothecary jars. When I was a little girl, my grandmother carried an old handkerchief with an embroidered honeybee on the corner and told me it reminded her "to work hard and be sweet." (Always a good one.) I decided to create my own rendition in the shape of a honeycomb. This tissue paper rainbow honeycomb is simple and adds a whimsical touch to any corner or doorknob.

HOW TO USE RAINBOW

When I first developed this project, I envisioned a rich spectrum of every single color of the rainbow. You can achieve that with the help of a rainbow tissue paper pack from the craft store. You cannot have too much packed in! Plus, the tissue creates such a lovely, luxurious quality, you won't want to skip out on colors.

(MATERIALS)

template (page 187)
white paper
scissors
rainbow tissue paper
glue stick
threading needle
100% polyester thread
ribbon

COLORS

all the colors

TIME

This American Life
(the Phil Collins breakup episode)

INSPIRATION

tissue honeycomb balls

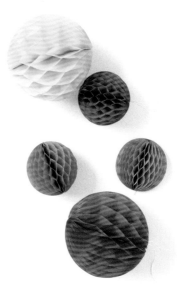

(INSTRUCTIONS)

1 Copy the template onto white paper, and cut out. Cut 8 sheets each of 18 colors of tissue paper so they are slightly larger than the template. Stack them in your preferred order.

2 Glue along all the A lines of the template. Lay down the first sheet of tissue paper. Glue along the B lines of the template. Lay down the second sheet of paper. Repeat until you have glued all the sheets.

3 Make sure everything is trimmed to the outside edge of the template.

4 Open the honeycomb and confirm that everything is glued appropriately. Thread a needle with a secure knot. Puncture a hole ¼ inch (6 mm) from the top edge of the template and pull the thread through all the glued sheets. Knot on the other side, leaving it just slack enough to allow you to reopen the honeycomb and spread it into a globe. Repeat on the other side of the template.

5 After sewing both sides of the stack, glue both ends of a ribbon to the bottom side of the template. Once the honeycomb is glued open, this will form the loop that you will use to hang it on a door, so make the ribbon long enough to allow it to hang to your desired height.

6 Glue the template to the last sheet of tissue. Note: Once you do this, the globe will be permanently open.

TIPS:

* *If you'd like to see a full rainbow spectrum on each side of the finished honeycomb, divide the sheets into two piles with four sheets per color, and follow the directions opposite for two stacks of glued sheets. When you complete step 3, glue the two sides together.*

* *For a cleaner edge, trim to the edge of the template after you glue down three to four sheets (as opposed to waiting until you've glued down everything).*

* *For more uniform honeycomb openings, mark your A and B guidelines along the straight edge of the template every two to three sheets. (As you stack more sheets on top of each other, the template will become harder and harder to see. By marking them again on the straight edge, you can know more exactly where to glue.)*

* *For precise honeycomb openings, make the glue lines quite thin.*

RAINBOW SCRAP CONFETTI

In crafting, as in life, the journey is just as important as the destination. That's why I save all my paper scraps along the way. They are often just as pretty as the project itself. As you might expect, rainbow crafts produce some of the loveliest scraps. Instead of trashing them, tuck them away and turn them into confetti. This would be particularly pretty for a wedding send-off or on the color wheel tablecloth on page 126.

HOW TO USE RAINBOW

If you're saving your scraps from other projects, you'll end up with a variety of rainbow colors. Combine shades of the same color in the same cup or separate out each one.

COLORS

all the colors!

TIME

a few episodes of *Saved by the Bell*, for old time's sake

INSPIRATION

sprinkles

(MATERIALS)

fringe scissors
paper scraps
scissors
metallic foil cupcake liners

(INSTRUCTIONS)

1 With fringe scissors, cut multiple vertical strips down one edge of the scraps.

2 Cut across the strips with scissors to create small squares.

3 Group together like colors in cupcake liners, or mix them up for a full rainbow spectrum.

RAINBOW BOOKS

Did you notice when the design world spoke out against boring bookshelves with the now-ubiquitous books-arranged-according-to-color system? Librarians have been silently protesting for years! I've tried out the technique, and although it's splendor for the eyes, it does not score points with other residents of the household—say, when my husband is looking for his English reference books. "One is in the red section, one is black, and shoot, I can't remember the other . . ." Here's my take: Create a vignette of rainbow books by painting the pages for some rainbow fun! I found a set of decorative books at the thrift store and had fun with colors. This vignette is more for the eyes as the paint glues the pages together.

HOW TO USE RAINBOW

I used a complete pastel rainbow—red, pink, orange, yellow, green, blue, purple—to offset the jewel tones of the book covers.

COLORS

pastel rainbow

TIME

an episode of *Freaks and Geeks*

INSPIRATION

rainbow bookshelves

(MATERIALS)

clamps
books
acrylic or house paint
foam paintbrush

(INSTRUCTIONS)

1   Clamp the pages of the books so they are pressed together tightly.

2   Paint the pages. You might need multiple coats to get the desired look. Allow each coat to dry completely before applying more paint.

RAINBOW PRINTABLE POP-UP CARD

I used to be a fantastic letter writer, but then the Internet happened, and these days my mail consists mainly of bills. It's not as much fun. As a remedy, I recently inducted myself into the Write More Letters Club (started just now). To be inducted, you (1) print off this card and (2) send it to a friend who could use some luck. Perhaps she just needs her pot of gold at the end of the rainbow!

COLORS

all the colors!

TIME

an episode of *I Love Lucy*

INSPIRATION

rainbow painting

(MATERIALS)

scissors

pencil

cardstock

2 pieces 11 by 17-inch
(28 by 43-cm) cardstock

bone folder

glue stick

(INSTRUCTIONS)

1. Download the two files for the card artwork.* Using a color printer, print the file that includes Pieces A and B (double sided) onto one white 11 by 17-inch piece of cardstock. Cut out using the light line around the inside perimeter of Piece B as a guide. Print the file that includes Pieces C and D (single sided) onto another 11 by 17-inch (28 by 43-cm) piece of cardstock, and cut out along the light line around the inside of the perimeter of the artwork.

2. Fold Piece B (the tree layer) along the light horizontal line located about 6 inches (15 cm) from the bottom of the piece.

3. Fold Piece C (the rainbow layer) at the base of the rainbow. Line up the bottom edge of Piece C with bottom edge of Piece B and glue with a glue stick.

4. Fold Piece D (the grass piece) along the light horizontal line located about 3 inches (7.5 cm) from the bottom of the piece. Line up the bottom edge of Piece D with bottom edges of Pieces C and B and glue with a glue stick.

5. Once all the pieces are glued together, fold down the elements and then make a vertical fold right down the middle. This will be the final size of the card.

---

* www.crafttherainbow.com/booktemplates

When I was living in Denmark, I returned home to the United States for a much-needed family visit. I also used it as an excuse to stock up on party and craft supplies for my newly established DIY website. At a local party store I came across raffle tickets in the most beautiful shades of sherbet. A roll of two thousand cost just a few dollars, so I bought one in each color. My mind was racing with potential uses. At one point I turned them into business cards by stamping them with my logo and contact information and handing them out like rewards from the skee-ball machine at Chuck E. Cheese. Eventually I realized how perfect they are for making garlands. You don't have the extra task of prepping new shapes because it is already done—just separate and sew! They are perfect for last-minute party décor.

CRAFT
THE
162
RAIN
BOW

HOW TO USE RAINBOW

I opted to leave out blue and purple, although the tickets come in a lovely periwinkle. As a variation, try it out with just one or two colors.

COLORS

bubblegum pink, deep berry, orange, sunshine yellow, mint green

TIME

an afternoon sewing and installing with friends to your favorite chill playlist

INSPIRATION

carnival tickets

(MATERIALS)

rolls of raffle tickets
sewing machine
tape, tacks, or hooks

(INSTRUCTIONS)

1   Tear apart the raffle tickets. I suggest making piles of each color and placing them in individual plastic bags for safekeeping.

2   Sew the tickets together down the middle in any color combination you desire. I sewed a pink, red, orange, yellow, and mint pattern down the middle horizontally. (Sewing horizontally allows them to flap around more.) I chose a zigzag stitch in a dark thread so it would stand out, but any stitch will do.

3   Hang at various heights using tape, tacks, or hooks.

TEMPLATES

Oversize Magnolia *enlarge 200 percent*

PINK, PAGE 26

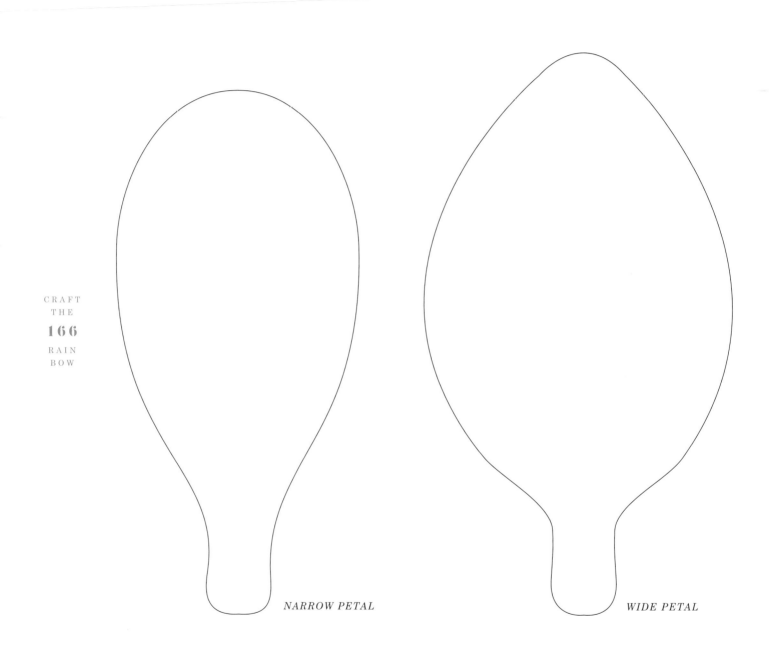

NARROW PETAL

WIDE PETAL

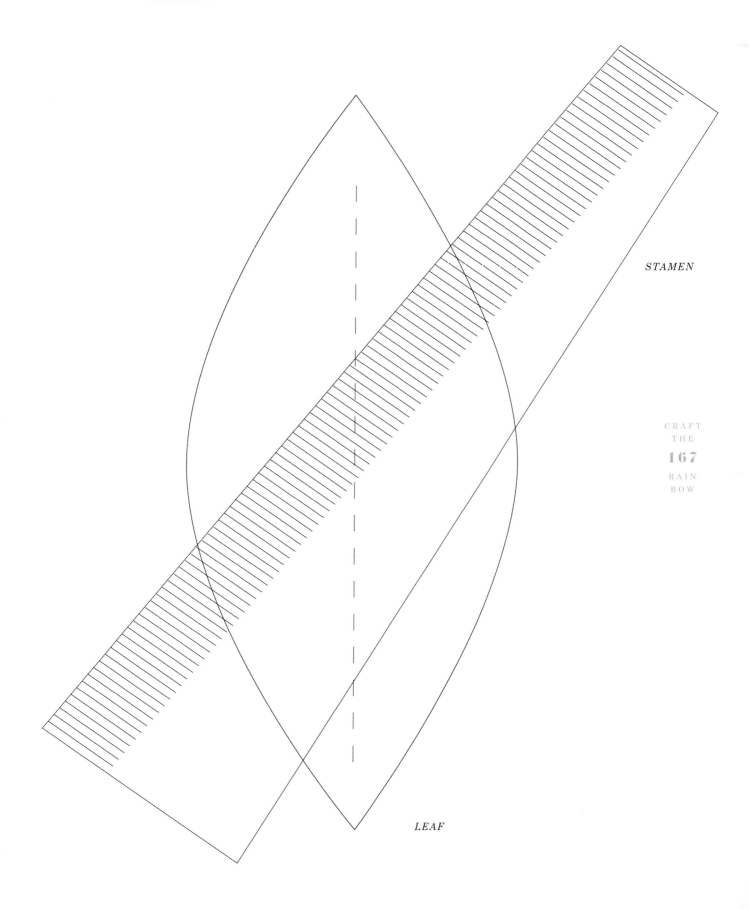

STAMEN

LEAF

Dala Horse Piñata *enlarge 400 percent*

RED, PAGE 38

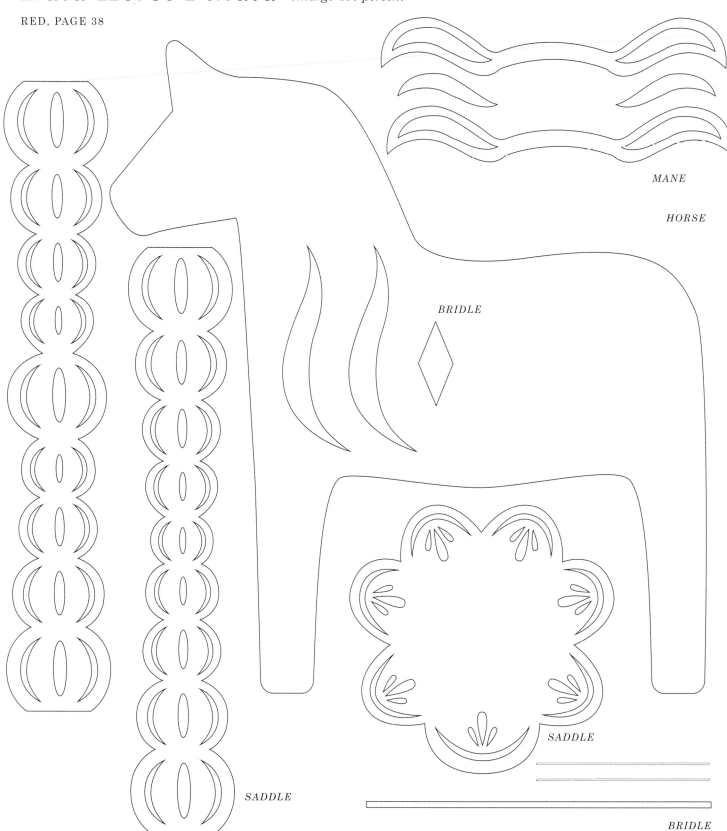

MANE

HORSE

BRIDLE

SADDLE

SADDLE

BRIDLE

SADDLE

Gemstone Folded Paper Lamp *with numbered guidelines*

RED, PAGE 46

Orange Swedish Garlands

ORANGE, PAGE 52

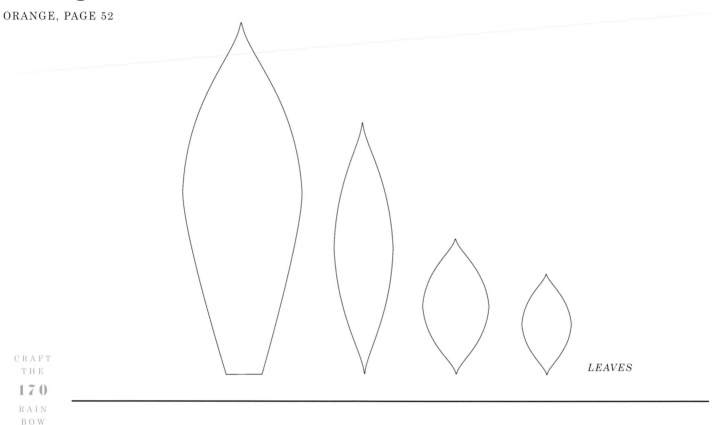

LEAVES

Balloon Arch with Paper Leaves

ORANGE, PAGE 58

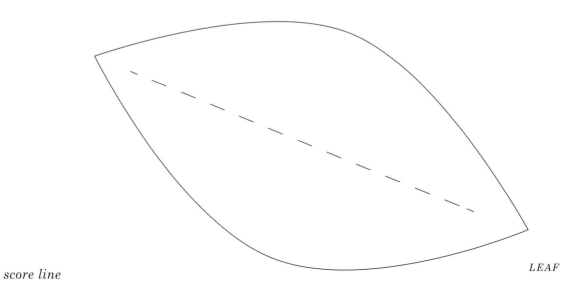

score line

LEAF

Paper Disk Bracelet

ORANGE, PAGE 56

DISK

Floral Himmeli Chandelier

YELLOW, PAGE 64

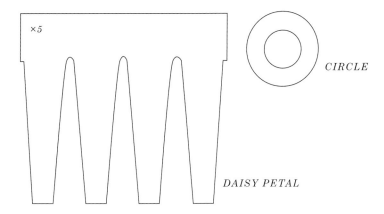

×5

CIRCLE

DAISY PETAL

Origami Money Lei

GREEN, PAGE 74

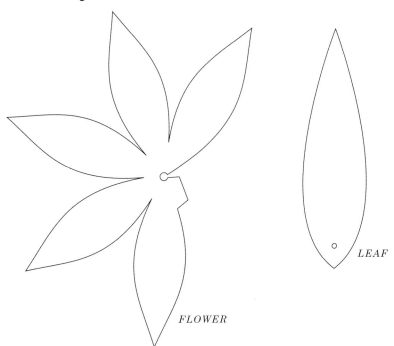

FLOWER

LEAF

Dip-Dyed Paper Flowers

BLUE, PAGE 86

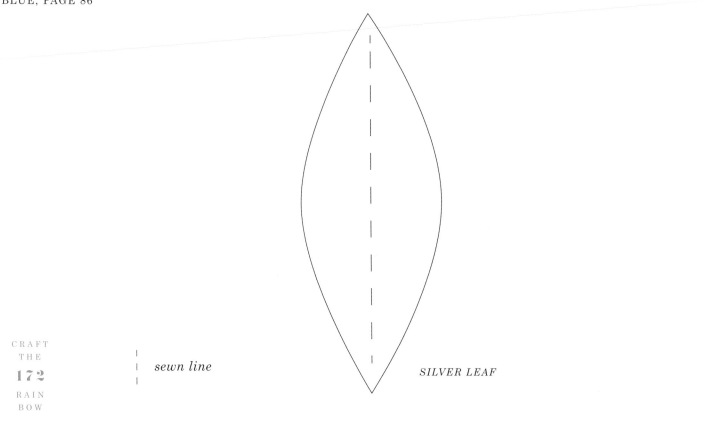

sewn line

SILVER LEAF

Paper Brooch and Earrings

BLUE, PAGE 92

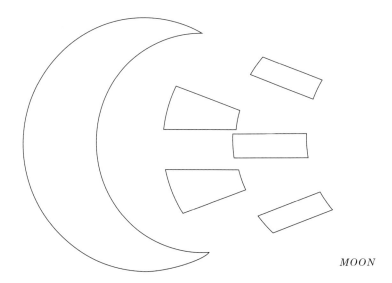

MOON

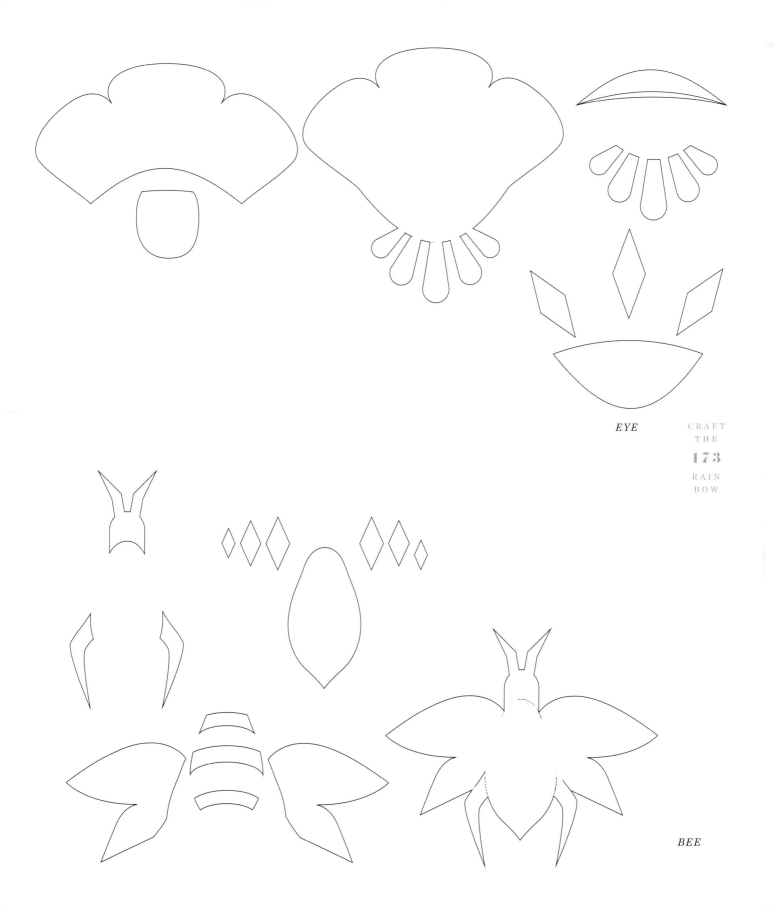

EYE

BEE

Floral Cutout Mobiles *enlarge 200 percent*

PURPLE, PAGE 96

White Paper Sculpture *enlarge 200 percent*

ARROWHEAD

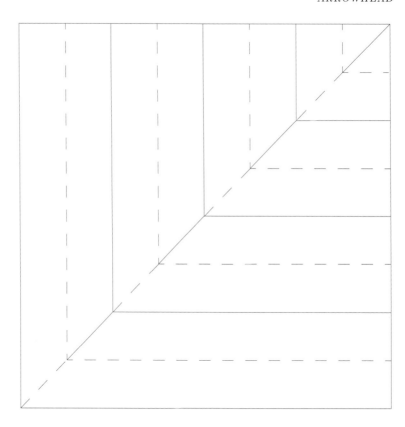

Dotted lines signify valley folds; solid lines signify mountain folds.

CHEVRON

Dotted lines signify valley folds; solid lines signify mountain folds.

SQUARE

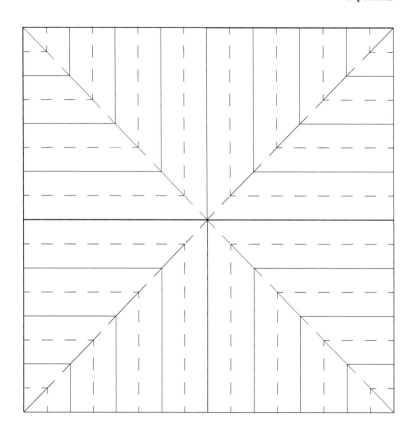

Dotted lines signify valley folds; solid lines signify mountain folds.

Holly-and-Berry Garland *enlarge 200 percent*

WHITE, PAGE 108

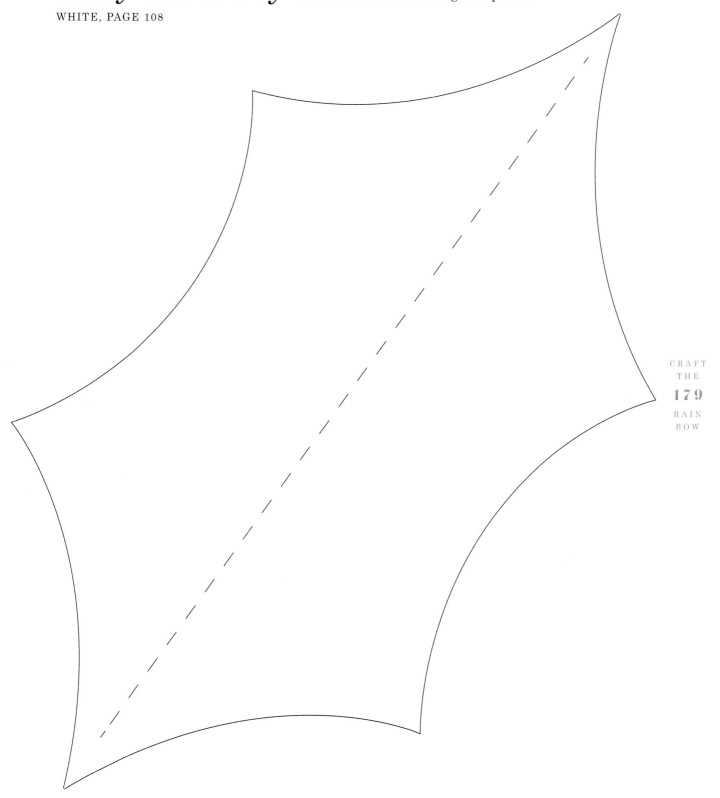

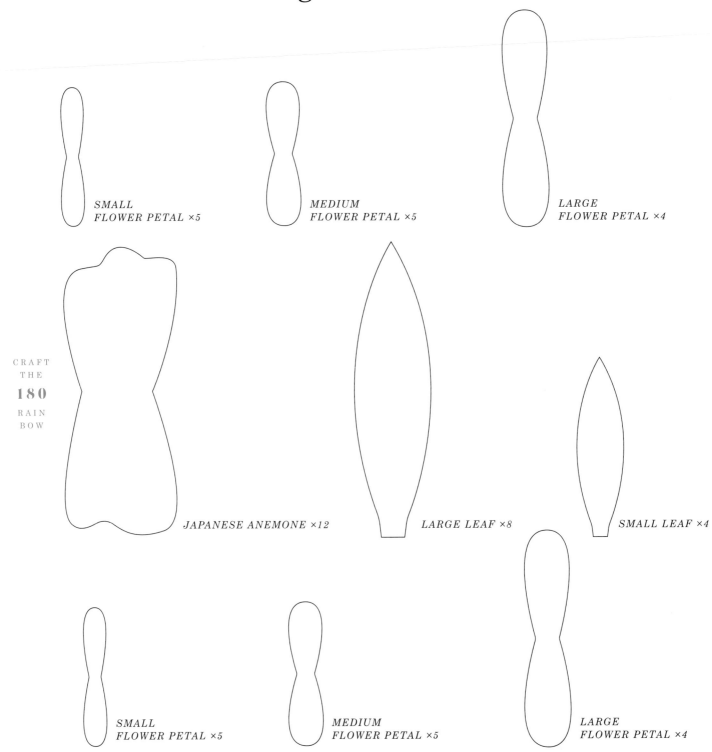

SMALL
FLOWER PETAL ×5

MEDIUM
FLOWER PETAL ×5

LARGE
FLOWER PETAL ×4

CRAFT
THE
180
RAIN
BOW

JAPANESE ANEMONE ×12

LARGE LEAF ×8

SMALL LEAF ×4

SMALL
FLOWER PETAL ×5

MEDIUM
FLOWER PETAL ×5

LARGE
FLOWER PETAL ×4

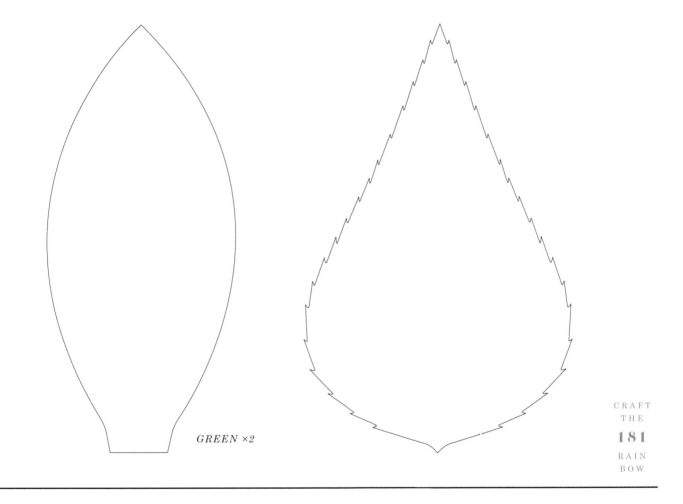

GREEN ×2

Rainbow Necklace RAINBOW, PAGE 128

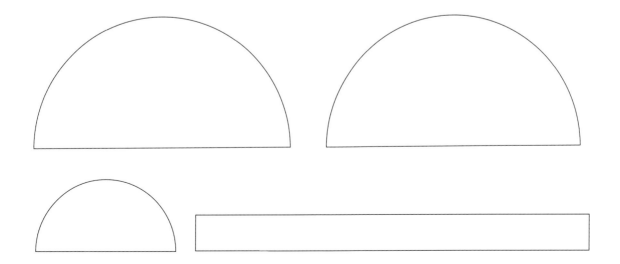

PRIMARY

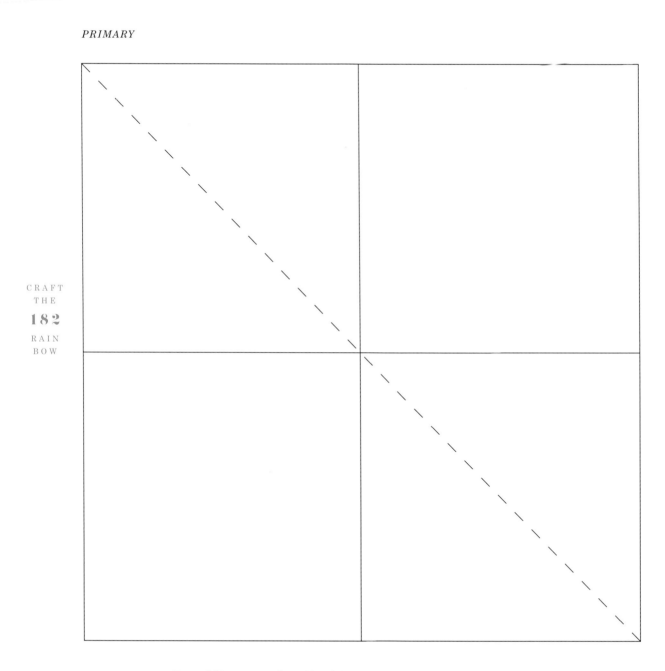

Dotted lines signify valley folds; solid lines signify mountain folds.

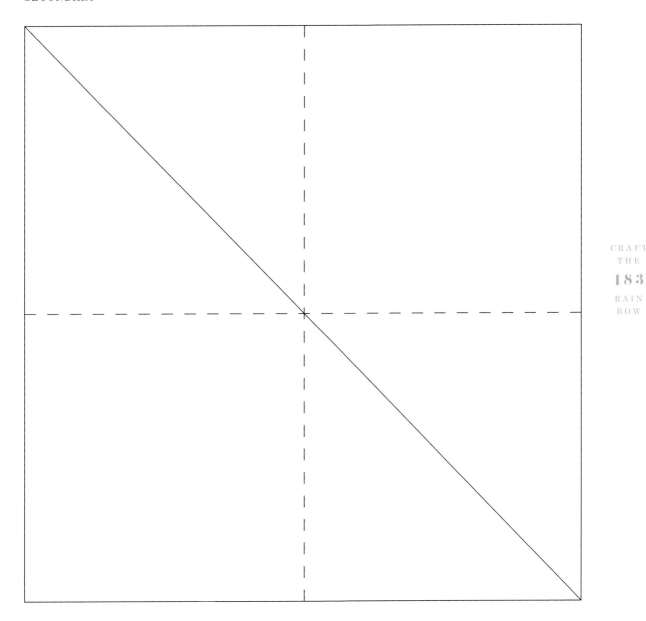

Dotted lines signify valley folds; solid lines signify mountain folds.

Rainbow Paper Plants

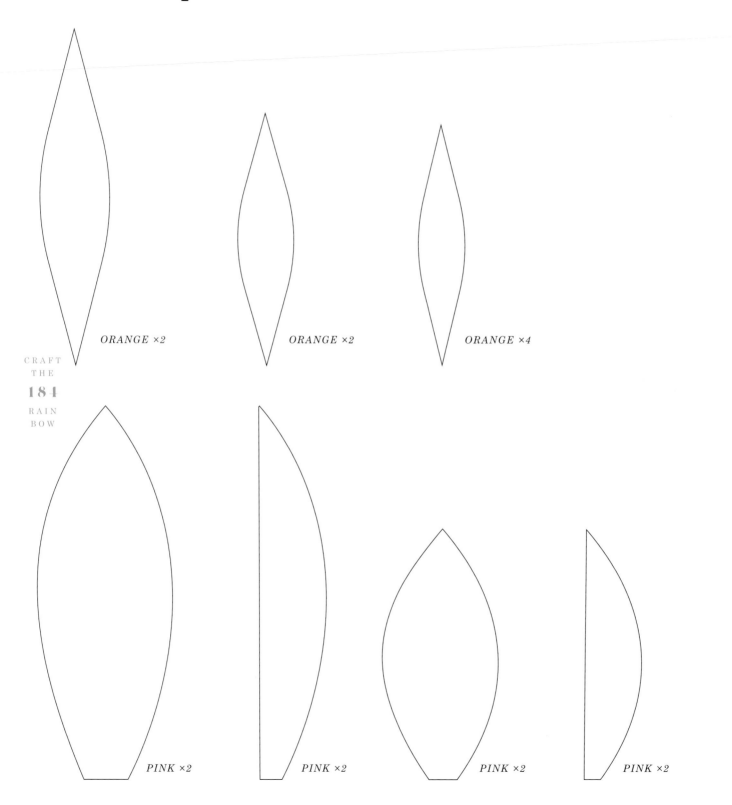

ORANGE ×2

ORANGE ×2

ORANGE ×4

PINK ×2

PINK ×2

PINK ×2

PINK ×2

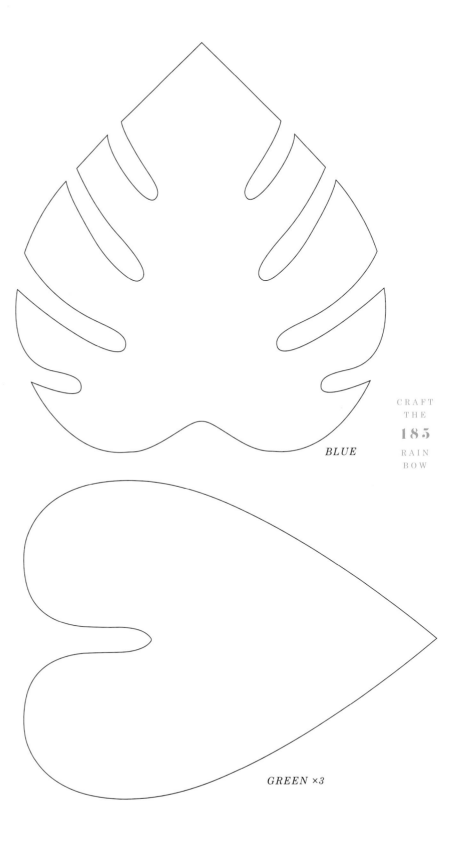

BLUE

PURPLE ×3

GREEN ×3

Flower Crown RAINBOW, PAGE 148

COLOR KEY

1. Coral
2. Pink
3. Purple
4. Blue
5. Yellow
6. Peach
7. White and blue

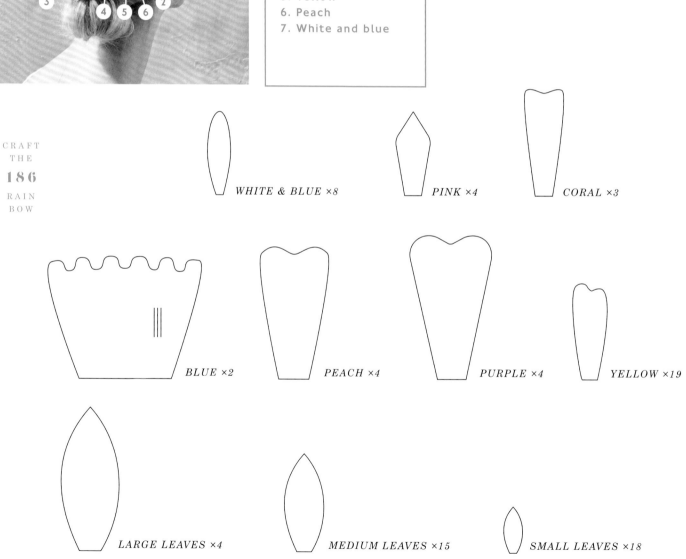

WHITE & BLUE ×8

PINK ×4

CORAL ×3

BLUE ×2

PEACH ×4

PURPLE ×4

YELLOW ×19

LARGE LEAVES ×4

MEDIUM LEAVES ×15

SMALL LEAVES ×18

Rainbow Honeycomb RAINBOW, PAGE 152

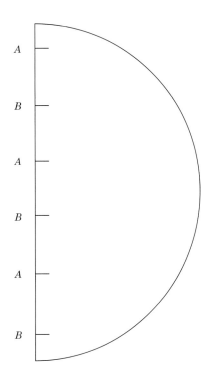

A

B

A

B

A

B

Party Goods Mandala GREEN, PAGE 79

MATERIALS KEY

1. Cup
2. Honeycomb tissue ball
3. Teardrop
4. Straw
5. Plate
6. 1½-inch (4-cm) paper circle
7. 3-inch (7.5-cm) paper circle
8. Honeycomb diamond
9. Palm tree food pick
10. Tissue paper fan
11. Party horn
12. Number candles
13. Plastic fork
14. Toothpick

RESOURCES

Thanks to the following for supplying items and support in the making of this book.

CRAFT SUPPLIES

- STUDIO CARTA
- EXQUISITE THREADS (on Etsy)
- SILK & WILLOW
- KNOT & BOW
- MY MIND'S EYE
- STAMPIN' UP!
- HELLO MAYPOLE
- MERMAID'S BEADS
- PICTURELINE (for seamless photography paper)
- HARMONY PROVO
- DARLYBIRD
- HAILEY LIECHTY

CREPE PAPER

- CARTE FINI
- LIA GRIFFITH
- CASTLE IN THE AIR
- D. BLÜMCHEN & CO.

PROPS/FURNITURE

- ANTHROPOLOGIE
- HUSET
- TERRAIN
- WEST ELM
- WAYFAIR
- CRATE & BARREL
- ABC HOME

WALLPAPERS AND BACKDROPS

- CALICO WALLPAPER
- CHASING PAPER
- DROP IT MODERN
- HYGGE AND WEST
- JUJU PAPERS
- FERM LIVING
- LAURA ASHLEY
- SANDBERG WALLPAPER
- REBEL WALLS

- ENGELSKA TAPETMAGASINET
- JESSICA ZOOB FOR ROMO BLACK EDITIONS

PARTY SUPPLIES

- MERI MERI
- OH HAPPY DAY PARTY SHOP
- SHOP SWEET LULU
- ZURCHERS
- POPPIES FOR GRACE

CLOTHING

- WHIT NY
- ASOS
- VAUX VINTAGE
- ANNIEOHVINTAGE
- SLEEPY JONES
- J.CREW
- ZARA

SERVICES

- SOIL AND STEM
- ANNIE BEE CAKERY

QUOTE CONTRIBUTORS

- JUSTINA BLAKENEY, *thejungalow.com*
- LISA CONGDON, *lisacongdon.com*
- SIBELLA COURT, *thesocietyinc.com.au*
- KATIE HATCH, *sleepyjones.com*
- DANIELLE KROLL, *hellodaniellekroll.com*
- EVA JORGENSEN, *sycamorestreetpress.com*
- NATALIE MILLER, *nataliemillerdesign.com*
- KENDRA SMOOT, *kendrasmoot.com*

ACKNOWLEDGMENTS

Lucky me had a generous parade of fairy godmothers turning pumpkins into carriages for this book. They not only helped to make it possible, but they also took it to a place I couldn't have imagined. Service in any form is my love language, and because this book required so much assistance, I have never felt so loved—and relieved—in all my life.

The success of a craft book is all in the minute details, and I was fortunate enough to have an ongoing team of interns and volunteers who made things happen by running errands, cutting, pasting, dyeing, and putting up with terrible recorder playing. Some of these included Jayne Verhaaren, Eliza Jackson, Tiffany Blake, Ana Wolfgramm, Anna Killian, Melissa Stewart, Taylor Smith, Michelle Larney, Alex Jameson, Katie Nuckols, India Hayes, Roxy Stanley, Hanne Giaquem, Laura Ann Atkin, Megan Allen, Julia Bigelow and family, Ally Price, and Alexis McKinnon.

Thanks to our lovely models, who were a delight to work with: Annie DeSantis, Alex Gunnell, Larissa Price, Anna Stevenett, Tiffany Blake, and Isabelle Aaron.

Thank you to a few others who lent their artistic expertise, like Tanner Williams and Shannon Petty of Ink Run Press. Aliza Wride provided top-notch wardrobe styling and general upbeat spirit. Rachel Kiser Jones lent her honed painting skills from afar. Danielle Wilson for providing custom-made creations. Nicole Land of Soil and Stem for bringing on gorgeous florals. Annie Larrabee of Annie Bee Cakery for bright and beautiful cakes. Thank you! Your work took it to another level.

Thank you to my creative friends and colleagues who shared their favorite colors with us: Justina Blakeney, Lisa Congdon, Sibella Court, Katie Hatch, Danielle Kroll, Eva Jorgensen, Natalie Miller, and Kendra Smoot.

Thank you to those who lent out their materials and homes: Hailey Liechty; Brook and Misty Walker of the infamous Pink House in Alpine, Utah; Rachelle Lynch; Wendy Ahlman of Chrysalis Preschool; and Zina Bennion for pointing me in the right direction. Richard and Debby Swan for constant encouragement and answering last-minute pleas for help.

I've been lucky to see my small blog grow into something much larger than I could have imagined. First up, thank you to Ashley Isenhour for coming on initially as an intern, then braving it as my first part-time employee. Thank you for taking a leap into the unknown as I figured out what in the world I was doing. Thank you for moving back just in time to save the day. I'm so glad to have your touch on this book. Second, to the Lars business director, Mary Nielson, for moving to Utah in the nick of time to put things in order. Without you, this book and the business wouldn't have happened so smoothly—or at all. Thank you for taking it all on and for crying when you saw the pretty pictures. More thanks to Rebecca Young, fellow Scandinavian and flower lover. I'm so glad we got you! Thank you for making this book your own and for lending out your instruments, your excellent modeling hands. Last, thank you to Anna Killian, who keeps Lars looking good by capturing beautiful tutorial photos.

To my agent, Judy Linden, for your encouraging words and support from the beginning. Thank you for guiding me to work with Shawna Mullen at Abrams, who believed in this project from the get-go and nurtured it along. Your calming influence was especially helpful under the pressure. Thank you also to Melanie Falick for your encouragement along the way. Deb Wood, thank you for turning the layout into magic.

Thank you to our photographer, Chaunté Vaughn. I was hoping for magic when you came on board, but my expectations were far exceeded. Thank you for inducing many tears of joy on set. And for playing Phil Collins on repeat. And for loving yellow as much as I do.

Thank you to Eva Jorgensen, Meta Coleman, Merrilee Liddiard, Alma Loveland, and Sarah Wright for your insight, encouragement, and friendship. Particular thanks to Merrilee for your revelatory brainstorm sessions and for loaning out your house. Thank you to Meta for getting as excited about the book as I was and lending out your styling expertise and props. Thank you to Mary Lee for listening, offering ideas, and supplying me with an endless supply of brass. When in doubt, brass.

Thank you to my family, who infused me with the desire to create. Special thanks to my sister, Caitlin Boyes, who stepped in to help out with a few projects, and my brother, Ryan, for late-night paintings and record/guitar jams.

And last, thank you to my husband, who didn't see his wife for a good portion of the year, but gave in every way he could. He painted floors, missed sleep, cooked lasagnas, and helped tame my absurd overuse of parentheses. With Paul, I've always felt freedom, loving support, and fierce loyalty.

Thank you to my readers, who have followed along over the years and allowed me to continue honing my craft. You've made this possible.

ABOUT THE AUTHOR

Brittany Watson Jepsen is a designer, a crafter, and the founder and creative director of the daily craft and design lifestyle blog *The House That Lars Built*, which includes various licensed product lines and a YouTube channel. Her work has been featured in the *New York Times* and Vogue.co.uk, and on the *Today Show* and CNN. She lives in Provo, Utah, with her husband. See more of her creations at TheHouseThatLarsBuilt.com.